"I love this book. One meets real ho... Lewis said it well when he quipped, ... dull. When one meets the real thing, ı ... ...chapters awakened within me a deeper hunger ... for righteousness. I pray it will cause those same hunger pangs to spread so that many more will taste and see that the Holy One himself is an irresistible treasure."

Jason C. Meyer, Pastor for Preaching and Vision, Bethlehem Baptist Church, Minneapolis

"The Reformed view of sanctification has resonated with me for a long time. More importantly, it is biblically rooted, realistic, and hopeful, and it doesn't fall into the error of perfectionism. Now we have a wonderfully accessible presentation of the Reformed view of sanctification. The scriptural support for a progressive view of sanctification is persuasively made. The realistic struggle that characterizes our lives is set forth, and the hope we have in Christ Jesus is proclaimed. I was encouraged and convicted in reading this work."

Thomas R. Schreiner, James Buchanan Harrison Professor of New Testament Interpretation, Southern Baptist Theological Seminary, Louisville

"A great combination of theological insight and practical advice on one of the most important of all Christian doctrines."

Douglas J. Moo, Wessner Chair of Biblical Studies, Wheaton College

"The Reformed and evangelical mind has recently concentrated much attention on the doctrines of justification and adoption, with many salutary effects. In some instances, however, concentration has degenerated into myopia, resulting in the distortion of the doctrine of sanctification. The present collection of essays is a helpful remedy to this situation. With chapters that are richly biblical, Christ-centered, and humane, *Acting the Miracle* refocuses our attention on the place and purpose of sanctification among the manifold works of the triune God. Readers will find this book both theologically and pastorally satisfying."

Scott R. Swain, Associate Professor of Systematic Theology and Academic Dean, Reformed Theological Seminary, Orlando

"This book is theologically informed and pastorally wise. It helpfully distinguishes and defines definitive and progressive sanctification, and it shrewdly shows how to approach Christian living without being reductionistic."

Andy Naselli, Assistant Professor of New Testament and Biblical Theology, Bethlehem College and Seminary, Minneapolis

Acting the Miracle

Other Desiring God Conference books:

Acting the Miracle

God's Work and Ours in
the Mystery of Sanctification

John Piper & David Mathis
general editors

Contributions by Kevin DeYoung, Ed Welch,
Russell Moore, & Jarvis Williams

 CROSSWAY
WHEATON, ILLINOIS

Cover design: Matt Naylor

First printing 2013

Printed in the United States of America

Unless otherwise indicated, Scripture quotations are from the ESV® Bible (*The Holy Bible, English Standard Version*®), copyright © 2001 by Crossway. 2011 Text Edition. Used by permission. All rights reserved.

Scripture quotations marked NASB are from *The New American Standard Bible*®. Copyright © The Lockman Foundation 1960, 1962, 1963, 1968, 1971, 1972, 1973, 1975, 1977, 1995. Used by permission.

Scripture references marked NKJV are from *The New King James Version*. Copyright © 1982, Thomas Nelson, Inc. Used by permission.

Scripture references marked NRSV are from *The New Revised Standard Version*. Copyright © 1989 by the Division of Christian Education of the National Council of the Churches of Christ in the U.S.A. Published by Thomas Nelson, Inc. Used by permission of the National Council of the Churches of Christ in the U.S.A.

All emphases in Scripture quotations have been added by the authors.

Trade paperback 978-1-4335-3787-5
PDF ISBN: 978-1-4335-3788-2
Mobipocket ISBN: 978-1-4335-3789-9
ePub ISBN: 978-1-4335-3790-5

Library of Congress Cataloging-in-Publication Data

Acting the miracle : God's work and ours in the mystery of sanctification / John Piper and David Mathis, editors.
  pages cm
  Includes bibliographical references and index.
  ISBN 978-1-4335-3787-5 (tp)
  1. Sanctification. 2. Spiritual formation. 3. Christian life.
I. Piper, John, 1946– II. Mathis, David, 1980–
BT765.A18 2013
234'.8—dc23   2013011772

Crossway is a publishing ministry of Good News Publishers.

VP		23	22	21	20	19	18	17	16	15	14	13
15	14	13	12	11	10	9	8	7	6	5	4	3	2	1

To Scott Anderson,
who pioneered our National Conference a decade ago,
serves as our host and emcee at Desiring God events,
leads the team daily as our executive director,
and weathers the waves of affliction,
"sorrowful, yet always rejoicing"
(2 Corinthians 6:10).

Contents

Contributors

Kevin DeYoung is pastor of University Reformed Church in Lansing, Michigan, where he has served since 2004. He is a council member of The Gospel Coalition and author of *Just Do Something: A Liberating Approach to Finding God's Will*, as well as (on the topic of sanctification) *The Hole in Our Holiness: Filling the Gap between Gospel Passion and the Pursuit of Godliness*. Kevin and his wife, Trisha, have five children (Ian, Jacob, Elizabeth, Paul, and Mary).

David Mathis is executive editor at Desiring God and an elder at Bethlehem Baptist Church, Minneapolis. He is a graduate of Furman University, Greenville, South Carolina, and is completing a distance degree with Reformed Theological Seminary. He is editor of *Thinking. Loving. Doing.: A Call to Glorify God with Heart and Mind* and *Finish the Mission: Bringing the Gospel to the Unreached and Unengaged*. He and his wife, Megan, have twin sons (Carson and Coleman).

Russell Moore is president of the Southern Baptist Ethics and Religious Liberty Commission. He is author of *Adopted for Life: The Priority of Adoption for Christian Families and Churches*, as well as *Tempted and Tried: Temptation and the Triumph of Christ*. He is married to Maria, and they have five sons.

John Piper is founder of and teacher for Desiring God and chancellor of Bethlehem College and Seminary in Minneapolis. For over thirty years, he was senior pastor at Bethlehem Baptist Church. He is author of over fifty books, including *Desiring God*, *The Pleasures of God*,

Don't Waste Your Life, *Seeing and Savoring Jesus Christ*, and (on the topic of sanctification) *Future Grace: The Purifying Power of the Promises of God*. John and his wife, Noël, have five children and twelve grandchildren.

Ed Welch is a faculty member at the Christian Counseling and Education Foundation (CCEF) and has been counseling for almost thirty years. He has written extensively on depression, fear, and addiction, and his books include *When People Are Big and God Is Small* and (most recently) *Shame Interrupted*. Ed and his wife, Sheri, have two married daughters and four grandchildren.

Jarvis Williams is associate professor of New Testament interpretation at Southern Baptist Theological Seminary in Louisville, Kentucky. He is the author of *One New Man: The Cross and Racial Reconciliation in Pauline Theology* and *For Whom Did Christ Die: The Extent of the Atonement in Paul's Theology*. He is married to Ana, and they have a son (Jaden).

Introduction

The Search for Sanctification's Holy Grail

David Mathis

Sanctification talk is notorious. If you've made the rounds in Christian circles for long enough, you know. You know.

Gather a dozen thoughtful, biblically and theologically informed Jesus followers. Steer the conversation in the direction of *sanctification*—*what* it is and *how* you pursue it practically. Then take a step back, watch, listen, and give it some time.

If you let the discussion go long enough, and it gets into just about any detail, you'll soon be able to discern a dozen distinct perspectives on the nitty-gritty of sanctification.

Opinions on sanctification are like elbows, some might say. *Everybody's got 'em.*

Sanctification Gets Personal

As much as any Christian doctrine, sanctification gets personal—indirectly when we talk about the *what*, and then in particular when we address the *how*. As soon as we're saying what sanctification is, it's inevitable that the lines soon must be drawn to how we live. And the more defensive we are about our way of life, the less open we tend to be about having Scripture revise our notions about sanctification.

At the level of definition, as John Piper will explain in more detail in chapter 1, the fancy English word *sanctification* is simpler than it sounds. It's built on the Latin word *sanctus*, meaning "holy." *Sanctification* is the modest theological term we Christians typically use to refer to the process of being made holy.[1] For the Christian, whose standard of perfect human holiness is Jesus, the God-man, sanctification is essentially becoming more like Jesus—"conformed to the image of his Son," as Romans 8:29 puts it.

Another way to talk about sanctification is Christian growth or maturation. It's a big word for the little-by-little progress of the everyday Christian life. It encompasses how every professing Christian should be living, where holiness is heading, how fast the progress should be, and how it happens in real life.

Look up. Can you see the controversies swirling overhead?

It's Just Complicated

Not only is it personal, but sanctification talk also gets prickly quickly because it immediately involves so many massive realities in the Christian worldview and their coming together in daily life: grace and works; law and gospel; faith and the Holy Spirit; Christian obedience and pleasing God; love and good deeds. The stakes are high. Weak spots in our theology will turn up, before long, in our understanding of sanctification. It doesn't take long before a wacky doctrine elsewhere begins to mess with our doctrine of holiness. True, Christian theology is a seamless garment, and every doctrine eventually relates to every other, but sanctification calls the question faster than the others and has the tendency to accentuate our problem areas.

But the fact that sanctification gets personal so quickly, and theologically complicated so fast, doesn't mean sanctification talk is to be avoided. On the contrary, it means that it's all the more important. We neglect careful, biblically informed reflection on this doctrine to our detriment, to the minimizing of our love toward others, and to the

---

[1] More below on "two types" of sanctification: definitive and progressive.

diminishing of the glory of God. Difficult as it can be, we must venture to speak about these things. We must talk sanctification.

Two Types of Sanctification

To make things a touch more complicated, the New Testament has two ways of talking about sanctification. For starters, we should clarify that this is a book mainly about the sanctification that theologians call *progressive*. Even though the biblical texts bear out two types, Christians throughout the centuries have found it most helpful in theological discussion to refer to the progressive type as simply "sanctification." But the Scriptures also teach us about a kind of sanctification we can call "definitive."

Definitive sanctification is the status of holiness we receive simultaneous with conversion and justification.[2] It is the setting apart of believers, reliant on the holiness of Jesus, such that even the most unholy of those who truly have faith can be considered "saints" (holy ones, Rom. 1:7 and 1 Cor. 1:2) because they are "in" Jesus, the Holy One. "Sanctify" is used in this definitive sense in Hebrews (9:13–14; 10:10; 13:12), as well as in Paul, who says to the Corinthians, "you were sanctified" (1 Cor. 6:11). It is this definitive sanctification that marks the clean break with sin we hear about in Romans 6:11 ("Consider yourselves dead to sin"), Galatians 2:20 ("I have been crucified with Christ"), and Colossians 3:3 ("you have died"), among other texts.

But sanctification is also progressive. We are increasingly "set apart" as we progress in actual holiness, which flows from the spiritual life we have in Jesus by faith. This is the way the term *sanctification* is typically used theologically, and this is the focus of this book.

Piper will add more in the first chapter, but for now, suffice it to say that we are aware of, and greatly appreciative of, the often overlooked

---

[2] Perhaps we should be clear here about what is meant by "justification." Justification is God declaring the believing sinner to be righteous, through faith alone, on the basis of Jesus's righteousness alone. For more on justification, see John Piper, *Counted Righteous in Christ* (Wheaton, IL: Crossway, 2003) and John Piper, *The Future of Justification* (Wheaton, IL: Crossway, 2007).

doctrine of definitive sanctification. We lament with David Peterson that "definitive sanctification is a more important theme in the New Testament than has generally been acknowledged,"[3] but for our purposes in this book, take *sanctification* in the normal theological parlance of progressive sanctification, unless otherwise noted.

Beware of Slogans

Because of the inherent complexity of sanctification, involving not only these two types but also all these moving pieces (Jesus's person and work, the Spirit's work, faith, our works, grace, law, gospel, obedience, and more), there is a great temptation to oversimplify things. Because sanctification with all its tentacles feels like an octopus larger than we can comfortably tame, we may prefer our own little theological house pets that we can train and remain captain of. It's nice to have a slogan that can keep it simple for stupid humans and make us feel like we're in control.

Enticing as it sounds—and convicting as it may be to hear about if you've tried it—the well of sanctification reductionisms soon runs dry. "Let go and let God"—it won't be long before that creates some problems. "Simply obey"—that won't do it either. Nor will attaining some "second work of grace." "Just get used to your justification"—attractive, yes, but there's another reductionism at work here.

It's as if we find the biblical data to be just too numerous and complicated, and what we really need is to search for sanctification's holy grail. *It must be out there somewhere—surely, there's some quick fix, some theological secret to discover, some doctrinal key that unlocks what holiness really is and how to have it.*

But if there's any key to sanctification, it's this: abandon your search for the key. At least abandon the search for a shortcut. Let your quest for the holy grail of sanctification end right here and right now

---

[3] David Peterson, *Possessed by God: A New Testament Theology of Sanctification and Holiness*, New Studies in Biblical Theology (Downers Grove, IL: InterVarsity, 1995), 14. Peterson's work highlights "the foundational importance of definitive sanctification" (13), and we would recommend his book as a fine place to begin in considering how definitive sanctification serves "as a basis and motivation for holy living" (14).

and commit to a sanctification not of *only*, but of *all*—all the Scriptures, all of Christian theology, all the Bible's salvific pictures, and, most ultimately, all of Jesus.

Simply Getting Used to Justification?

For one, let's take a reductionism prevalent in the broadly Reformed community with which many readers of this book associate: the holy grail of justification by faith alone. One Lutheran spokesman, whom some Reformed would happily echo, says that sanctification is "simply *the art of getting used to justification*."[4]

Just off several years' fighting back a fresh assault on justification from various new perspectives on Paul, this precious doctrine, which became the occasion for Martin Luther to pioneer a sorely needed reformation, has become especially dear to many of us. So justification as a silver bullet for sanctification is enticing to those of us who love double imputation, Jesus's "alien" righteousness, and making much of God's free grace toward the ungodly.

The best possible meaning of such a slogan would have in view not just justification but the full panoply of initial and ongoing graces applied to the believer at the outset of the Christian life—new birth, faith and repentance, justification, definitive sanctification, adoption, and more. It would be better to say that progressive sanctification is based on definitive sanctification. Christian growth means learning to live like who we already are in Jesus, living out in and through us the holiness that is already ours in him.

But even on this best possible reading, there is so much more to be said, and this epithet for sanctification ends up betraying a sloppy understanding of justification or sanctification or both. Justification by faith alone is a beautiful, wonderful, essential doctrine, worth defending to the death. If we had the space, I'd love to give some extended ef-

---

[4] Gerhard Forde, "The Lutheran View," in *Christian Spirituality*, ed. Donald L. Alexander (Downers Grove, IL: InterVarsity, 1988), 13; emphasis original.

fort here to celebrating this vital doctrine. True Christian theology can't do without it and must not minimize it in any way. It is an essential aspect of our relationship to Jesus. But it's not the whole. The Scriptures have much more to say to us than simply *get to know your justification.* That way of saying it is careless at best, if not tragically misguided. What we need for practical sanctification is not one Christian doctrine, but all of them. Not one or a handful of Christian Scriptures, but every one. Not part of Jesus, but the whole Christ.

Union to the Rescue?

In response to such a reductionistic fixation on the doctrine of justification, a fresh wave of voices claim to have found the grail in another place, perhaps even more pious than justification, believe it or not. They rightly emphasize the reality and importance of our union with Christ. The best of these voices will not play union over and against justification, but note that union with Christ is "the big category" for the Holy Spirit's application of Jesus's redemptive work to us and that justification, sanctification, regeneration, adoption, and glorification are "aspects" of our union with Jesus by faith. Yes.

Since union with Christ "may be the most important doctrine you've never heard of,"[5] and since sanctification is one aspect of our union with Christ, it may be helpful here not to assume your familiarity but to provide a brief introduction to this important doctrine.[6]

Simply put, *union with Christ* is the theological term for the believer's being joined to Jesus by the Holy Spirit through faith. In fulfillment of God's ancient promise, *I will be your God, and you will be my people*, it is "the most general way of characterizing Jesus's work of

---

[5] Kevin DeYoung, *The Hole in Our Holiness: Filling the Gap between Gospel Passion and the Pursuit of Godliness* (Wheaton, IL: Crossway, 2012), 94.
[6] There's not enough space here to say all that should be said about union with Christ and its relevance and importance for sanctification. For more, see, among others, chapter 43 in Wayne Grudem, *Systematic Theology* (Grand Rapids, MI: Zondervan, 1994, 2000), 840–850; chapter 4 in Anthony Hoekema, *Saved by Grace*, (Grand Rapids, MI: Eerdmans, 1989, 1994), 54–67; and especially chapter 11 in Sinclair Ferguson, *The Christian Life: A Doctrinal Introduction* (Edinburgh: Banner of Truth, 1981), 104–14; as well as Ferguson's chapter "The Reformed View," in *Christian Spirituality: Five Views of Sanctification*, ed. Donald L. Alexander (Downers Grove, IL IVP Academic, 1989), 47–76.

salvation."[7] The way in which all that Jesus accomplished for us gets applied to us is through our being connected to Jesus, our being "in" him. The occasion of this connection is faith, and the agent of this connection is the Holy Spirit. Our union with Jesus is part and parcel of the covenantal relationship between Jesus and his bride in which the two become one—and what God truly has joined together, no man may separate.

Again, our faith union with Jesus is how the objective accomplishments of his life, death, and resurrection two millennia ago come to be subjectively applied to other humans, whether Peter, Paul, Mary, Augustine, Luther, Spurgeon, or believers in the twenty-first century. John Murray memorably captures this important distinction of the objective and subjective in the title of his book *Redemption: Accomplished and Applied.*[8] Our redemption was accomplished by Jesus in the past, and it is applied to us by the Spirit in our present.

Keep these two categories clear: Jesus's objective achievement and our subjective reception by faith through the Spirit. To put it simply and generally, our union with Jesus by faith is the way in which all that he has purchased for us is given to us. Specific aspects, then, of this general union include regeneration, justification, sanctification, adoption, and glorification. In a book on sanctification, it is important to see that sanctification is one aspect of our union with Jesus, alongside other vitally essential aspects.

Joined to Jesus

The apostle Paul alone references our being "in Christ" in some form over 160 times. Draw in the apostle John and his own way of saying it, and you have well over two hundred references, in just these two writers, of believers' being "united" to Jesus.

The two prevailing ways in which the New Testament speaks of our

---

[7] John Frame, *Systematic Theology* (Phillipsburg, NJ: P&R, forthcoming), n.p.
[8] John Murray, *Redemption: Accomplished and Applied* (Grand Rapids, MI: Eerdmans, 1955).

union with Jesus are (1) our being *in him*, and (2) his being *in us*. Paul says in Ephesians 1:3 that it is "in Christ" that Christians have "every spiritual blessing in the heavenly places"—including sanctification—and that the Father "chose us *in him* before the foundation of the world" (v. 4). In 2 Corinthians 5:17 Paul says, "If anyone is *in Christ*, he is a new creation." He says in Philippians 3:8 that he has "suffered the loss of all things and count[s] them as rubbish, in order that I may gain Christ and be found *in him*." It is "in him" that we "become the righteousness of God" (2 Cor. 5:21), and only "in Christ Jesus" do we have "wisdom from God, righteousness and sanctification and redemption" (1 Cor. 1:30).

But union with Christ means not only that we are "in him," but also that he is "in us." Paul writes in Romans 8:10, "If Christ is *in you*, although the body is dead because of sin, the Spirit is life because of righteousness," and he declares in Galatians 2:20, "I have been crucified with Christ. It is no longer I who live, but Christ who lives *in me*." When Paul challenges the Corinthians, "Examine yourselves, to see whether you are in the faith," he tells them, "Test yourselves. Or do you not realize this about yourselves, that *Jesus Christ is in you*?" (2 Cor. 13:5). In Colossians 1:27 he celebrates "the riches of the glory of this mystery, which is *Christ in you*, the hope of glory."

Since union with Christ means not only that the believer is "in" Jesus but also that Jesus is "in" him, it should be no surprise to find several passages from John that combine both ideas.

> By this we know that *we abide in him and he in us*, because he has given us of his Spirit. (1 John 4:13)

> Whoever feeds on my flesh and drinks my blood *abides in me, and I in him*. (John 6:56)

The classic passage may be from John 15. In the words of Jesus,

> Abide in me, and I in you. As the branch cannot bear fruit by itself, unless it abides in the vine, neither can you, unless you abide in me.

I am the vine; you are the branches. Whoever abides in me and I in him, he it is that bears much fruit, for apart from me you can do nothing. If anyone does not abide in me he is thrown away like a branch and withers; and the branches are gathered, thrown into the fire, and burned. If you abide in me, and my words abide in you, ask whatever you wish, and it will be done for you. (John 15:4–7)

The Help and the Hitch of Union with Christ

So there's just a taste of the bigness and biblical prevalence of union with Christ. But the specific topic before us is sanctification. So let's make some connections. Sinclair Ferguson claims, "Of all the doctrines surrounding the Christian life this, one of the profoundest, is also one of the most practical in its effects."[9] How is it that the doctrine of union with Christ is so practically helpful in our progressively becoming like Jesus?

Again here's Ferguson:

When we are joined to him there is also a sense in which his life and power become available to us to transform our lives. We may even go as far as to say that when we are united to Christ, the whole of his past life is made available to us, not simply to compensate for our past (by way of pardon) but actually to sanctify our present lives, so that our own past may not inescapably *dominate* our present Christian life. We, who in the past have marred the image of God by sin, may gaze into the face of Christ and discover that the power of our own past sin may not destroy us in the present.[10]

There is a fullness in our union with Jesus that provides a richness of resources for our blessing and worship and growth. There is a multi-dimensionality to this union, as it is fleshed out in its various aspects, that meets us where we are in our process of becoming more like Jesus and helps move us forward.

And there's more. This is Anthony Hoekema:

[9] Ferguson, *The Christian Life*, 114.
[10] Ibid, 111.

One of the ways in which the doctrine of union with Christ is helpful is in enabling us to preserve a proper balance between two major aspects of the work of Christ: what we might call the *legal* and the *vital* aspects. The Western branch of the Christian church, represented by such theologians as Tertullian and Anselm, tended to emphasize the "legal" side of Christ's work. . . . The Eastern wing of the church, however, represented by such theologians as Irenaeus and Athanasius, was more inclined to stress the "vital" or "life-sharing" side of Christ's work.[11]

Union with Christ helps us to see and be reminded that Jesus isn't just our righteousness but also our holiness—he is "the Holy and Righteous One" (Acts 3:14). And he is not just our holiness but also our life. And he isn't just our life but also our righteousness. Union reminds us to embrace the whole Christ for all his benefits rather than just picking a favorite and crafting a slogan. You can't have him for justification without having him for sanctification.

So this often neglected but practically powerful doctrine of the believer's union with Jesus is vital for sanctification. Then have we found our silver bullet? Was the warning above about avoiding sanctification sloganeering and reductionisms issued prematurely? Might union with Christ be the holy grail?

Here's the hitch. Union with Christ ends up being a very nondescript way of talking. Perhaps you're already sensing this from what I've written (or not written) in this introduction. As theologian John Frame observes, union with Christ is "the most general way of characterizing Jesus's work of salvation. . . . [It is] an exceeding broad topic."[12] It's a glorious generality and is meant by God to be gloriously general, but it doesn't carry inherently the specificity of its various aspects—regeneration, justification, sanctification, adoption, glorification. Indeed, as Frame says, union with Christ and being "in" Christ "are the most general things that can be said about us as [God's] people."[13] The way in which we flesh out in more detail what it means to be united to Jesus

[11] Hoekema, *Saved by Grace*, 66.
[12] Frame, *Systematic Theology*.
[13] Ibid.

is to address the blessings of justification, sanctification, regeneration, and glorification. The strengths and weaknesses of union lie in its being the broad category that includes the other benefits. And the strengths and weaknesses of sanctification lie in its specificity as an aspect of that union. We mustn't play the two off each other. So where to from here?

Room for Reliance

As important and helpful as the doctrine of union with Christ is, this one doctrine is not sanctification's holy grail. We're back to a sanctification of *all*, not *only*. We return to the truth that what is needed for Christian sanctification is not some silver-bullet doctrine or fresh slogan or new overriding emphasis, but the whole of the Bible and the whole of Christian theology and the whole of Jesus. The same Jesus who is our righteousness for justification *is* the same Jesus who is our holiness for sanctification—both definitive and progressive—*is* the same Jesus we're united to by faith to receive those priceless graces.

By virtue of our Spirit-powered faith union with Jesus, we have the new-creation spiritual life of regeneration, and the righteousness of justification, and the holiness of sanctification, and the familial affection and privilege of adoption, and the honor of glorification. This is big. It gets complicated. There are so many ducks that it's hard to get them all in a row—and that's just the way God would have it. After all, he is the sanctifier, not we. He would rather we always lean on him for holiness than supposing we have it figured out.

Where's the Spirit in All This?

Before closing this introduction, it's worth asking, *What is the role of the Holy Spirit in all our talk about sanctification?* Sometimes our sense of fairness is irked by how often Jesus and the Father get mentioned while the Holy Spirit seems to remain out of view. This may not be all bad.

It can be helpful to think of the Spirit as the self-effacing member of the Trinity. In John 16:14, Jesus describes the main "job" of the Spirit this way: "He will glorify me." There is something intrinsically mystical about the Spirit, as John 3:8 intimates: "The wind blows where it wishes, and you hear its sound, but you do not know where it comes from or where it goes. So it is with everyone who is born of the Spirit." Graham Cole, even in writing a long book about the Spirit, acknowledges this elusiveness:

> What God has made known concerning the divine name, will, and ways we know truly but not exhaustively. As for the Spirit, the mystery deepens. For . . . the Spirit points away from himself to another. Thus there is an elusiveness about the Spirit when thematized as the object of inquiry.[14]

As there is a sense of the mystical and elusiveness to our union in Christ, so also with the Spirit who effects and sustains that union. In particular, the Spirit is elusive and self-effacing by relentlessly drawing attention to Jesus's person and work. So "the power of the Holy Spirit" (Rom. 15:13; see also 15:19; 1 Cor. 2:4; Eph. 1:16) often is known explicitly by other terms, such as "the power of the gospel" (see Rom. 1:16). It's not as though the gospel as a mere message has an inherent power apart from the power of the personal Spirit. The reason there is power in the gospel is that the Holy Spirit works through that Jesus-glorifying message.

So also "the power of the cross" (see 1 Cor. 1:17, 18, 24). In and of itself, the cross, or any news about a cross, isn't powerful. But God himself, in the particular person of the Holy Spirit, possesses power and has chosen to do his most direct and potent work in and through and alongside the preaching of a crucified Messiah, who was dead and is now alive. Which brings us at last to the great goal of sanctification.

The Beginning and End of Sanctification

The beginning and end of Christian sanctification is none other than Christ himself. There is an initial relationship with Jesus that first sets us

---

[14] Graham Cole, *He Who Gives Life: The Doctrine of the Holy Spirit*, Foundations of Evangelical Theology (Wheaton, IL: Crossway, 2007), 52.

apart as definitively sanctified and gets the gears going for progressive sanctification, but a deepening relationship with Jesus is the heart of sanctification, and knowing Jesus is the great goal of our sanctification. Jesus is not only the preeminently sanctified one and the one who empowers our sanctification by his Spirit, but also he is the one whom the whole of our sanctification is shaping us to know forever. Knowing Jesus drives us onward in sanctification now (Phil. 3:8), and knowing Jesus is the eternal life that sanctification fits us for (John 17:3).

The greatest blessing of salvation is not mere forgiveness. It's not just justification and being declared righteous. It's not new birth. It's not even sanctification. It's not just the privilege of being united to him, but being united to him serves the greater goal of enjoying him. The greatest blessing of redemption is Jesus himself. All aspects of the Spirit's subjective application to us and all of Jesus's objective accomplishments for us conspire to this one great end: knowing Jesus, enjoying Jesus, admiring Jesus, and treasuring Jesus for all eternity.

This, as our contributors develop in the chapters ahead, is the very essence of holiness. Happiness in Jesus is not just the product of holiness; it is the essence of true Christian holiness.

Slogans will eventually lead us astray. Quick fixes won't last. What we need for Christian sanctification is all of the Christian Scriptures, and all of Christian theology, and ultimately all of Christ. We need all of Jesus—all his words, all the glorious doctrinal truths about him, all his divine life, all his full humanity, all his lived-out righteousness, all his death for us, all his resurrection power, all of his help for us in the Holy Spirit. Without a great Jesus as the center of our now and forever, there is no great salvation.

What's Ahead

This book had its start in the Desiring God 2012 National Conference on the theme of sanctification. About 2,500 of us gathered in Minneapolis and dedicated the weekend to considering this important theme and its countless implications for everyday life.

The chapters in this book began as plenary addresses at the conference and have been carefully revised and expanded for publication by our authors (most of whom are more writers than speakers). We gave the conference to the topic of sanctification because we saw a need. One of our hopes in this book is to kindly and carefully correct some of the misstatements about sanctification we've heard and some of the unwise trajectories we see, but our primary aim is to positively construct a vision for what Christian sanctification is and with that to courageously venture some answers to the *how* questions, even though it's sure to raise some ire.

In the first chapter Piper seeks to "put sanctification in its place" by expanding on this introduction in terms of both defining sanctification and developing its relationship to the whole of the process of salvation. Chapter 2 is Kevin DeYoung's important treatment of the multiplicity of motivations in sanctification. DeYoung provides a rich exposition of Colossians 3 that aims to point us toward the full Christian deck of resources available for our growth in holiness while avoiding our tendency to fixate on one.

Ed Welch kindly agreed to put his lifetime of study and experience to our service in chapter 3. We asked how physical limitations and disabilities affect our sanctification, and Welch responded with this especially useful primer on the embodied soul, including several real-life stories to flesh it out. If you're short on time, you may just want to jump straight to Welch's chapter. It is very good.

We knew that discussing this theme and making it practical meant raising many issues and concerns beyond the daily means of grace but also that the spiritual disciplines must be addressed in the course of the discussion. Jarvis Williams tackles the personal means of grace in chapter 4 (focusing on Bible intake, prayer, preaching the gospel to yourself, and suffering), while Russell Moore deals brilliantly with the corporate dynamics in Christian sanctification in chapter 5—a chapter you may find worthy of a re-read and extended reflection.

Finally, in the last chapter, Piper brings it all together. He continues his work from chapter 1 and picks up on the work of the other chapters in pressing the theology into everyday life. Piper gets practical in addressing how God works in and through us to bring about actual holiness in our lives through conscious trust in what he's revealed about himself and his specific promises to us.

Our prayer is that God would be pleased to make use of these chapters in both orienting you and fueling your fire for acting the miracle of Christian sanctification.

1

Prelude to
Acting the Miracle

Putting Sanctification in Its Place

John Piper

This chapter has two parts. In the first part, I try to define sanctification. In the second part, I try to put it in its place in the process of salvation. In this way, I hope to set the stage for the other chapters to come in this book.

1) What Is Sanctification?

The English word *sanctify* or *sanctification* is built on the Latin word *sanctus*, which means "holy." In English, we don't turn the adjective *holy* into a verb. The world *holify* does not exist. But in the Greek language of the New Testament, the adjective *holy* (*hagios*) *can* be made into a verb (*hagiazō*), which means "to make holy" or to "treat as holy." In Greek, that same adjective for *holy* (*hagios*) can be made into three different nouns (*hagiosmos*, *hagiōsunē*, *hagiotēs*), which sometimes mean "the condition of being holy" ("holiness") or "the process of becoming holy"—which would be "holification" if such a word existed in English, but since it doesn't, we use "sanctification."

Here's the crucial point: *any time you read in the New Testament any form of the word "sanctify," you know you are reading about holiness.* So a book like this on sanctification is a book on being or becoming holy. And the reason I use the terms "being" or "becoming" holy is that the New Testament refers to our holiness in both of those senses—a condition of being holy and a process of becoming holy.

Being Holy

The clearest place to see both of these in one chapter is Hebrews 10. Hebrews 10:10 says, "By [God's] will we have been sanctified through the offering of the body of Jesus Christ once for all." So there is a sense in which all those who believe in Jesus "have been sanctified." They *are* holy. And then four verses later (v. 14) we read, "By a single offering he has perfected for all time those who are *being sanctified*." So there is a sense in which Christians are both perfected already (are perfectly holy) and are being sanctified (being made holy).

Both the condition of being holy and the process of becoming holy are prominent in the New Testament. Neither is minimized. The most obvious way to see the prominence of the Christian condition or state of holiness is to see that Paul calls Christians "saints" forty times in his thirteen letters. Paul's favorite name for Christians is *saints*. The New Testament word behind the English "saint" is simply the adjective for "holy" turned into a noun—"holy ones" (*hagioi*). You can see the connection between the condition of being sanctified and the name "saints" in 1 Corinthians 1:2: "To the church of God that is in Corinth, to *those sanctified* (*hēgiasmenois*) in Christ Jesus, *called to be saints* (*klētois hagiois*)." So the picture is that God calls us, and unites us by faith to Jesus, so that "in Christ Jesus," we are holy, sanctified, and the name that we get, therefore, is "saints" or "holy ones."

Becoming Holy

But the process of becoming holy (sanctification) is also prominent in the New Testament. We saw Hebrews 10:14, "By a single offering he has perfected for all time those who are *being sanctified*." We see it in

2 Corinthians 7:1: "Let us cleanse ourselves from every defilement of body and spirit, *bringing holiness to completion* in the fear of God." So if we are bringing holiness to completion, there is a process of becoming fully holy. We are not there yet. Or 1 Thessalonians 5:23: "Now may the God of peace himself *sanctify you completely*." This prayer shows that our becoming holy is not yet complete. So Paul asks God to complete it. Or Hebrews 12:10: "[Our earthly fathers] disciplined us for a short time as it seemed best to them, but [God] disciplines us for our good, *that we may share his holiness*." So a fuller holiness is coming through God's discipline.

The upshot of all this so far is that whenever the New Testament talks about sanctification, it is talking about holiness. And when it is talking about *our* holiness, it is either talking about the *condition* of our *being* holy (because we are in Christ Jesus—and thus saints), or it is talking about the *process* of our *becoming* holy through God's work in our lives.

Holiness as a Family Trait

That's the first part of our answer to the question, *What is sanctification?* But notice what we've done. We have pushed the question back to another question, *What is holiness?* Or what does it mean to *be* holy and *become* holy? And it seems to me that the most important thing in defining *our* holiness is to notice its connection to *God's* holiness. For example, 1 Peter 1:14–16 says, "As obedient children, do not be conformed to the passions of your former ignorance, but *as he who called you is holy, you also be holy* in all your conduct, since it is written, 'You shall be holy, for I am holy.'"

So the basis of God's command that his people be holy is that he is holy. Peter explains this not as an arbitrary demand but as a family trait. "As obedient *children* . . . be holy in all your conduct." Peter is thinking the same way the apostle John is in his first letter, when he says, "No one born of God [that is, who has God as his Father] makes a practice of sinning, for God's seed abides in him, and he cannot keep on sinning because he has been born of God. By this it is evident who are the children of God, and who are the children of the devil: whoever does not practice righteousness is not of God" (1 John 3:9–10). The command to "be holy" is a command to show that we are God's seed. We have his spiritual DNA, the genetic code of his holiness. That is, we are his children.

This is exactly confirmed by the words of Hebrews 12:10 that we just looked at a moment ago: "[Our earthly fathers] disciplined us for a short time as it seemed best to them, but [God our heavenly Father] disciplines us for our good, *that we may share his holiness.*" It's not a contradiction to say, on the one hand, that we share in God's holiness because we are born of God (and have his spiritual DNA, as it were, his genetic code of holiness), and to say, on the other hand, that God must discipline us so that we share in his holiness. If a child is to grow into the fullest expression of his Father's character, he needs both the DNA by virtue of birth and the practice of that character with the help of his father's discipline. In other words, we need regeneration by God's seed, and we need sanctification by God's Spirit—in order to grow up into the full participation in his holiness.

Or here's the way Paul puts it. We need a "new self"—a new man, a new creation—"created after the likeness of God in true . . . *holiness*"; and we need to "*put on*" that new holy self (Eph. 4:24). In other words, Christians *are* holy and must *become* holy. We have the seed of God's likeness (God's holiness) imparted to us when we are born again, and we must grow into that likeness (that holiness) to show who our Father really is. "By this it is evident who are the children of God, and who are the children of the devil: whoever does not practice righteousness is not of God" (1 John 3:10). "As obedient children, . . . 'be holy for I am holy'" (1 Pet. 1:14–16) "[Our Father] disciplines us for our good, that we may share his holiness" (Heb. 12:10). "If you are left without discipline . . . then you are illegitimate children and not sons" (Heb. 12:8).

So, in asking the question, *What is holiness?* and in seeing that the holiness we need is to share in God's holiness, the question now becomes, *What is God's holiness?*

The Holiness of God

The root meaning of the Old Testament word for holy (*chadōsh*), where the biblical idea starts, is the idea of being separate—different and separated from something and devoted to something else. When applied to God, that meant God's holiness is his separateness, his being in a class by himself, and thus being supremely valuable in every way. You can see this meaning of holy in these illustrations:

> When Moses struck the rock instead of speaking to it the way God said, God said to him, "Because you did not believe in me, *to uphold me as holy* in the eyes of the people of Israel, therefore you shall not bring this assembly into the land that I have given them." (Num. 20:12; see 27:14). In others words, Moses treated God not as separate from man, and thus supremely trustworthy, but as a mere man along with others whose word could be ignored.

> Or in Isaiah 8:12–13, God says to Isaiah, "Do not call conspiracy all that this people calls conspiracy, and do not fear what they fear, nor be in dread. But the LORD of hosts, him *you shall honor as holy.* Let him be your fear, and let him be your dread." In other words, don't lump God into the same group as all your other fears and dreads. Treat him as an utterly unique fear and dread and set apart from all the ordinary fears and dreads.

God's Transcendent Completeness and Self-Sufficiency

So here is how I conceive of the holiness of God. God is so separate, so above, and distinct from all else—all that is not God—that he is self-existent and self-sustaining and self-sufficient. Thus he is infinitely complete and full and perfect in himself. Since God is separate from, transcendent above, all that is not God, he was not brought into existence by anything outside himself. He is self-existent. He depends on nothing for his ongoing existence and so is self-sustaining. And therefore he is utterly self-sufficient. Complete, full, perfect.

The Bible makes plain that this self-existing, self-sustaining, self-sufficient God exists as three divine persons in one divine essence. Thus the Father knows and loves the Son perfectly, completely, infinitely; and the Son knows and loves the Father perfectly, completely, infinitely. And the Holy Spirit is the perfect, complete, infinite expression of the Father's and the Son's knowledge and love of each other. This perfect Trinitarian fellowship is essential to the fullness and perfection and completeness of God. There is no lack, no deficiency, no need—only perfect fullness and completeness and self-sufficiency.

But Something's Missing

This is the holiness of God: his transcendent completeness and self-sufficiency.[1] But there is a missing dimension in that description of holiness. Because God is utterly unique and self-existent, there is nothing besides God except what God wills to create. Therefore, God is absolute value. He is absolute worth. His transcendent completeness makes him infinitely valuable. Of infinite worth. It's necessary to introduce this dimension of holiness into the definition because the Bible presents God's holiness in terms of morality as well as terms of transcendence. Holiness is not just otherness. It is good and pure and right.

Introducing God's infinite worth helps us conceive of God's holiness in moral categories. Before creation, there were no standards of goodness and righteousness outside of God that could be used to say, *God is good or right according to these standards.* All there was was God. So, when there is only God, how do you define *good*? How can

[1] Jonathan Edwards makes the connection between God's self-sufficiency and holiness like this: "God, being infinite in power and knowledge, he must be self-sufficient and all-sufficient; therefore it is impossible that he should be under any temptation to do any thing amiss; for he can have no end in doing it. . . . So God is essentially holy, and nothing is more impossible than that God should do amiss." Jonathan Edwards, "The Sole Consideration, That God Is God, Sufficient to Still All Objections to his Sovereignty," in *The Works of Jonathan Edwards*, vol. 2 (Edinburgh: Banner of Truth, 1974), 107. What I am doing in what follows is asking, *What does "amiss" mean for a Being who has no law above his own nature to which he must conform and which could define "amiss"?*

there be holiness with a moral dimension, and not just a transcendent one?

My answer is this: the moral dimension of God's holiness is that every affection, every thought, and every act of God is consistent with the infinite worth of his transcendent fullness.[2] In other words, I am defining holiness not only as the infinite worth of God's transcendent fullness but also as the harmony that exists between the worth of that transcendent fullness and all God's affections, thoughts, and acts. That harmony is the beauty of holiness.

In sum, then, God is transcendent in his self-existent completeness; and is, therefore, of infinite worth; and there is perfect harmony between the worth of his transcendent completeness and all his affections, thoughts, and acts. This is God's holiness. Or to shorten it even more: his holiness is his transcendent fullness, his worth, and the beautiful harmony of all his acts with that worth.[3]

So when God says in 1 Peter 1:16, "Be holy, for I am holy," or when Hebrews 12:10 says, "He disciplines us . . . that we may *share his holiness*," what aspects of his holiness do they mean? Not that we should be transcendent as God is transcendent. Nor that we should be self-existent as God is self-existent. But, rather, that in all our affections and thoughts and acts, we, like God, should be a beautiful harmony with the infinite worth of God.

Human Holiness

So I would define human holiness as feeling and thinking and doing only what is consistent with God being the supreme and infinite trea-

[2] Here's Jonathan Edwards's way of saying this: "*God's holiness* is his having a due, meet and proper regard to everything, and therefore consists mainly and summarily in his infinite regard or love to himself, he being infinitely the greatest and most excellent Being. And therefore a meet and proper regard to himself is infinitely greater than to all other beings; and as he is as it were the sum of all being, and all other positive existence is but a communication from him, hence it will follow that a proper regard to himself is the sum of his regard." Jonathan Edwards, *The "Miscellanies" (Entry Nos. 833–1152)*, in *The Works of Jonathan Edwards*, vol. 20 (New Haven, Yale University Press, 2002), 460.
[3] Stephen Charnock uses a quaint phrase to say something similar. God's holiness is that he "works with a becomingness to his own excellency." *The Existence and Attributes of God*, vol. 2 (Grand Rapids, MI: Baker, 1979), 115.

sure of the universe. Our holiness is our conformity to the infinite worth of God. The opposite of holiness is sin, which is any feeling or thought or act that shows that for us God is not the beautiful treasure that he truly is.

This leads me then to define the process of sanctification as *the action by which we bring our feelings and thoughts and acts into conformity to the infinite and all-satisfying worth of God*. And I realize that I just said, "the action by which *we* bring our lives into conformity to the worth of God." No doubt, I could have said, "the action by which *God* brings our lives into conformity to the worth of God." Or better, *both*. That too is what this book is about. *Who does it? And how is it done?* We have much work to do.

2) What Is the Place of Sanctification in the Process of Salvation?

With that definition of sanctification before us, we now ask, *What is the place of sanctification in relation to the other works of God in our salvation?* To do so, we look at Romans 8:28–30:

> And we know that for those who love God all things work together for good, for those who are called according to his purpose. For those whom he foreknew he also predestined to be conformed to the image of his Son, in order that he might be the firstborn among many brothers. And those whom he predestined he also called, and those whom he called he also justified, and those whom he justified he also glorified.

So here we have one great sequence of God's saving acts. Starting in verse 29, God foreknows, God predestines, God calls, God justifies, and God glorifies. The question is: *Where is sanctification in that sequence, and how does it relate to the other works of God?*

Where's Sanctification?

The answer is: it is in the beginning as the goal of predestination, and it is at the end as an essential part of glorification. And in between there are two works of God that make it possible for spiritually dead, wrath-deserving sinners to be sanctified—calling and justification. So let's look very briefly at the beginning and the end and these two works in the middle.

Verse 29: "Those whom [God] foreknew he also predestined to be conformed to the image of his Son, in order that he might be the first-born among many brothers." God predestines a group of people to be conformed to the image of his Son. In other words, he predestines our sanctification, our holiness. Here's the way Paul says it in Ephesians 1:4–5: "He chose us in him before the foundation of the world, that we should be holy. . . . He predestined us for adoption as sons through Jesus Christ."

Our Destiny: Holiness

The reason God has chosen a people for himself is to give them a particular destiny, and that destiny is their holiness, their sanctification, their conformity to Jesus Christ, the Son of God. The aim of this conformity to Christ (according to Romans 8:29) is "that he might be the firstborn among many brothers." This means two things. It means that our being changed into the likeness of Jesus is because we are brought into the family and given a family likeness with God as our Father and Jesus as our brother. The other thing it means is that Jesus is not just another brother but the unique "firstborn" who is exalted and worshiped by his brothers.

From the very beginning, God predestined that his people would be sanctified, that is, that they would be transformed into the likeness of his Son. Or, we can say, we were predestined to share the Son's holiness, and in that holiness be able to see him and celebrate him as we ought.

Glorification Includes Sanctification

But not only do we see sanctification at the beginning in this sequence in Romans 8:29 but also at the end in verse 30: "Those whom he justified he also glorified." You might ask, "Why didn't Paul say, 'Those whom he justified he also sanctified, and those whom he sanctified he also glorified'?" One of the reasons Paul didn't say that is that "glorification" includes sanctification. Paul thinks of glorification beginning in this life as we are incrementally changed into the likeness of the all-glorious Christ.

Here's 2 Corinthians 3:18: "We all, with unveiled face, beholding the glory of the Lord, are being transformed into the same image from one degree of glory to another. For this comes from the Lord who is the Spirit." We are being transformed into the same image from glory to glory. This is the very transformation into the image of the Son that Romans 8:29 was talking about. Sanctification is the beginning of glorification. We move from one degree of conformity to Christ to the next, that is, one degree of glory to the next.

Beholding Is Becoming

Just as seeing him through a glass darkly in this life means we are sanctified incrementally, the day will come, according to 1 John 3:2, when we will see him as he is. "Beloved, we are God's children now, and what we will be has not yet appeared; but we know that when he appears we shall be like him, because we shall see him as he is." *Beholding is becoming.* Partially now. Completely later. We usually call it *sanctification* now. And we will call it *glorification* then. But they are all one process.

Now between predestination and glorification, Paul mentions calling and justification. Romans 8:30: "Those whom he predestined he also called, and those whom he called he also justified, and those whom he justified he also glorified." Without these two works of God, sinners who are spiritually dead and who deserve the wrath of God could never be sanctified. Without God's call, we would be dead and unresponsive to all his sanctifying influences. And without God's justification, we would be found guilty as charged, and there would be no sanctifying influences but only wrath. So without divine calling and divine justification, there would be no sanctification.

The Work of God's Call

The call of God can be either his general invitation to the whole world to come to Christ or his particular, effective call that creates what it commands. When Paul says in verse 30, "Those whom he called he also justified," we know it does not mean God's general invitation. It's not true that all whom he invited he justified. He justifies only those who believe. The calling of God brings about the faith that we need to be justified. This is not a general call but a specific effectual call, like the call Jesus gave to the dead Lazarus: "Come forth." The call produced what it commanded.

Here's a description of God's effectual call from 1 Corinthians 1:22–24: "Jews demand signs and Greeks seek wisdom, but we preach Christ crucified, a stumbling block to Jews and folly to Gentiles, but to *those who are called*, both Jews and Greeks, Christ the power of God and the wisdom of God." The general call goes out to all Jews and Gentiles. "Come to Christ the crucified!" But not all come. To many the cross is folly; to others it is a stumbling block. But to those who are called, that is, those in whom God makes his call effective, their eyes are opened, and they see the cross not as foolish but as the wisdom of God and the power of God. This call is virtually the same as the new birth, regeneration. And without it, no one would be justified, because no one would believe. And no one would be sanctified because no one would have life.

The Work of Justification

But when God calls like this, faith in Jesus is awakened and by that faith we are justified—such that Paul can say, "Those whom he called, he justified," because the call creates the faith that justifies.

So the call of God removes one barrier to our sanctification, namely, our spiritual deadness. Justification removes the other great barrier to sanctification—and that barrier is our guilt in the courtroom of God and the just wrath of God resting on us (John 3:36). If God's wrath is resting on us because of our guilt, then we are not going to be sanctified.

God's remedy for this barrier is the great work of justification. He puts Christ forward by his perfect obedience, climaxing in his death, vindicated by his resurrection, and then offers this Christ to be received by faith. He promises that whoever believes will have pardon for all his sins and the imputation of Christ's perfect righteousness. Because of that pardon and that imputation we are declared not guilty but righteous. We are justified.

"As by the one man's [Adam's] disobedience the many were made sinners, so by the one man's (Christ's) obedience the many will be made righteous" (Rom. 5:19). "For our sake he made him to be sin who knew no sin, so that in him we might become the righteousness of God" (2 Cor. 5:21; see also Phil. 3:9). All this is by faith alone, apart from works of the law. "For by works of the law no human being will be justified in his sight, since through the law comes knowledge of sin" (Rom. 3:20). "For we hold that one is justified by faith apart from works of the law" (Rom. 3:28).

The Place of Sanctification

Putting it all together, from all eternity God has been holy—transcendently self-sufficient, of infinite worth, acting in beautiful harmony with the greatness of his worth. In that holiness, he foreknew a people for himself and predestined them to share his holiness—to be conformed to the image of his Son for the glory of his Son—and those whom he thus predestined for holiness, he called out of spiritual deadness into life and awakened saving faith, and those whom he thus called he justified so that all his wrath would be removed from us and there would be only mercy. All those whom he thus justified he is bringing from one degree of glory to another by his Spirit who dwells in us. His success in this work of sanctification is so certain that it is as good as done. Those whom he justified, he glorified.

The place of sanctification is embedded in the sequence of divine acts from eternity to eternity that infallibly come to pass. All whom he foreknew, he infallibly predestined. All he predestined, he infallibly called. All whom he called, he infallibly justified. All he justified, he will infallibly pursue with sanctifying grace till everyone is glorified.

2

Incentives for Acting the Miracle

Fear, Rewards, and the Multiplicity
of Biblical Motivations

Kevin DeYoung

My aim in this chapter is to correct a problem, and the problem is this: believing, preaching, praying, counseling, and self-diagnosing as if there was only one proper motivation for holiness. My concern is that as we try to help people on the journey of sanctification, we not unnecessarily limit ourselves. I fear we too quickly remove some of the tools from our sanctification tool belt. We set aside some of the weapons of our warfare. We flatten the promises and commands and warnings of Scripture, so we no longer allow ourselves to say all that the Bible would have us say.

Jesus is our great physician. Like any good doctor, he knows how to write different prescriptions for different illnesses. He has many doses at his disposal. He understands unique personalities and sins and situations. He is gracious to come at us in his Word—with all sorts of truth, for all sorts of people, from all sorts of angles—to keep us striving after holiness. Jesus has many medicines for our motivation.

Different Injuries, Different Applications

When I'm away from home, my wife usually calls at night to fill me in on the day. One night not long ago, my wife called me to talk about bees. She said there were all sorts of bees outside chasing the children. She tried to get them out, but one bee had disappeared into our three-year-old son's shirt. Suddenly he started screaming, "The bee! The bee! It's in my shirt!" So, like a good mom, she ripped off his little shirt, threw it down, and started stomping it with all her might. "Stupid bee!" my wife cried defiantly. "Stupid bee!" But the damage was done. Our youngest son, the one with lots of allergies, had been stung in the back. "I gave him as much Benadryl as the law allows," she related on the phone. That's what you do when your three-year-old gets a bee sting. You pump him full of allergy medicine.

That's not what you would do on all occasions (though parents will tell you there are worse ideas than loading your kids up with Benadryl). When your child is stung by a bee, you give him some drugs, hold him on your knee as long as he likes, and whisper in his ear, "It'll be okay, love. It'll be okay." But when the same son storms in the house, apoplectic from a tiny scrape on his knee, you tell him to buck up and go back outside. Good parents, like good doctors, understand that different injuries call for different application.

I think back to the days when I ran track and cross country in high school. Whenever I had an injury, the student trainers would tell me the same thing. Whether I had a hip flexor or shin splints or a sprained ankle or a lacerated spleen, they always told me to "ice it and take a couple ibuprofen." That was that. I wanted an X-ray or a CT scan or a replacement foot or something. But they didn't wander far from home. If you could be fixed with ice and ibuprofen, they had the prescription for you. If not, you were out of luck.

Good doctors know how to give different prescriptions to different patients. That's my point. My fear, however, is that when it comes to the care of souls, we get locked into a solitary prescription and stick with it no matter what. We tend to find one true, good, helpful biblical motivation for holiness and make that the equivalent of ice and ibuprofen.

Let me give you a few examples.

Duty Is Not Enough

Duty is one of the motivations that's true but often unhelpful all by itself. It's a biblical word, so we should not be afraid to use it. Jesus tells us in Luke 17:10, "So you also, when you have done all that you were commanded, say, 'We are unworthy servants; we have only done what was our duty.'" And Ecclesiastes 12:13 concludes: "The end of the matter; all has been heard. Fear God and keep his commandments, for this is the whole duty of man." We have an obligation to keep God's commandments because he is God and we are not. That's duty, *and* it's not a bad word. But it's usually not all God says. Normally, when God comes at us with commands, he says more than, "Listen up. I am the Lord your God. So start obeying." He comes with a multiplicity of motivations.

Think of the Ten Commandments. God doesn't simply give us a list of commands. He motivates with promises, threats, and theology.

- He starts by saying "I'm the Lord your God. *Your* God. I brought you out of Egypt. Do not worship anything or anyone else. I'm the God who saved you."
- He says, "Don't bow down to graven images." Why? "Because I'm a jealous God. I will visit your sins to the third and fourth generation if you disobey, but show steadfast love to thousands of generations if you love me and keep my commandments."
- He says, "Do not take the name of the LORD your God in vain, for he will not hold you guiltless." In other words, you'll have trouble on your hands if you ignore this one.
- He says about the fourth commandment in Exodus, "Observe the Sabbath day because God rested on the seventh day." And in Deuteronomy: "Take a break. Give your people a break because you were slaves once too. So don't be treating your servants like they're slaves." Both iterations contain motivations for obedience.

- He says, "Honor your father and mother, that it may go well with you." Here too we see God promising blessing for those who obey.

Even with the Ten Commandments, God does not resort to duty alone. He offers many reasons and incentives for obeying his commands.

Gratitude Is Not Enough?

Gratitude is another one of the biblical motivations that should not be made the be-all and end-all of our sanctification. I belong to the Reformed tradition and embrace the Heidelberg Catechism, which is known for its three sections of guilt, grace, and gratitude. I believe that in Romans 12:1 where Paul says, "I appeal to you . . . by the mercies of God, to present your bodies as a living sacrifice," he's harkening back to all of the promises in Romans 1–11 and inviting us to live a gratitude-informed life of faith. We see in Ephesians 5:4 that there should be "no filthiness nor foolish talk nor crude joking, which are out of place, but instead let there be thanksgiving." Gratitude helps to squeeze out what is mean and bitter and nasty. So whatever problems you may have as an angry person, one of your problems is a gratitude problem. It's entirely appropriate to connect gratitude with the struggle for sanctification.

But gratitude by itself is not enough. It can quickly turn into a debtor's ethic where we think, "All that I have has been given to me by God, so now I must live the rest of my life trying to pay him back." If we talk only about gratitude, we end up looking backward at God's blessings and never forward in faith toward his promises. Duty is fine. Gratitude is good. But they aren't enough all by themselves.

Justification Is Not Enough

Let me give you one final example, and this one may hit even closer to home. As important as justification is for the Christian, it's not meant to be the only prescription in our pursuit of holiness. Without a doubt, it is gloriously true that we are accepted before God because of the work of Christ alone, the benefits of which we receive through faith

Incentives for Acting the Miracle   47

alone, by grace alone. That ought to be our sweet song and confession
at all times. Justification is enough to make us right with God forever,
and it is certainly a major motivation for holiness. If we are accepted
by God, we don't have to live for the approval of others. If there is no
condemnation in Christ Jesus, then we don't have to fear the disap-
pointment of others.

There's no doubt that justification is fuel for our sanctification. But
it is not the only kind of fuel we can put in the tank. If we only remind
people of our acceptance before God, we will flatten the contours of
Scripture and wind up being poor physicians of souls.

Think of James 4:1: "What causes quarrels and . . . fights among
you?" James does not say, "You're fighting because you have not come
to grips with your acceptance in the gospel." He says, in effect, "You're
at each other's throats because you're covetous and you're selfish. You
want things that you don't have. You're demanding. You're in love with
the world. You're envious. That's what's going on in your heart right
now." Now, we might try to connect all that with a failure to believe
the gospel, but that's not what James says. He blames their quarrels on
their love of the world.

You have only to be a parent for a short time to see that people sin
for all sorts of reasons. Lately we've been using the excellent book *Long
Story Short* for our morning devotions with the kids. When we came
to the story of Cain and Abel, the book suggested a little lesson where
you hand a ten-dollar bill to one child but not to the others. Then you
ask the kids, "What would your response be if I gave your sister ten
dollars because she did something very pleasing to me, and I gave you
nothing?" The aim of the lesson is to relate to Cain's envy toward Abel.
So I just asked the question, and my son, in whom there is no guile, re-
plied without hesitation, "Daddy, I'd punch you in the stomach." Now
what's going on in his heart at that moment? Is his most pressing need
to understand justification, or is there a simpler explanation? I think
that my son at that moment, like the people James was addressing, was

ready to fight because of covetousness. He saw ten dollars, thought of the Legos he could buy with it, and was willing to do whatever he had to, to get what he wanted.

The problem with much of our thinking on sanctification is that we assume people are motivated in only one way. It's similar to the mistake some of those associated with Christian psychology fall into. They assume a universal-needs theory. They operate from the principle that everyone has a leaky love tank that needs to be patched up and filled up. If people could only be loved in the right way, they'd turn around and be loving people. Well, I don't doubt there is some commonsense insight there. But does the theory explain everyone? Is this the problem with Al-Qaida or Hamas—they all have leaky love tanks? Or are some other issues at play?

I have no problem acknowledging that sin is always an expression of unbelief. But there are a lot of God's promises I can disbelieve at any moment. Justification by grace alone through faith alone is not the only indicative I can doubt. I can disbelieve God's promise to judge the wicked or his promise to come again or his promise to give me an inheritance or his promise to turn everything to my good. These are all precious promises, each one a possible remedy for indwelling sin. To remind each other of justification is never a wrong answer. It is a precious remedy, but it is not the only one.

Colossians from the Sky

I've tried to make the negative case that there is no single, solitary biblical motivation for holiness. Now let's see the positive case for the multiplicity of motivations.

In Colossians 3 we see a staggering array of motivations for holiness. The first part of the chapter, verses 1–17, gives a macro-level view of how God motivates us. It deals with general commands, foundational principles. And in the last part of the chapter—the household code in verse 18 and following—we get the micro-level view that zeroes in on the family and day-to-day life. We'll start with the big picture before moving into the nitty-gritty where God gives specific motivations for specific commands.

Full of Imperatives

The first thing to notice is that this passage is full of imperatives. Paul wants the Colossians to live a certain way. He doesn't assume that by telling them the good news of the gospel, life transformation will automatically happen. He tells them what a Christian life should look like. Just look at the commands in chapter 3:

- Verse 2: "Set your minds on things that are above."
- Verse 5: "Put to death . . . what is earthly." That means immorality, impurity, evil desire, idolatry, and covetousness.
- Verse 8: "Put them all away," which includes anger and wrath and malice and slander and obscene talk.
- Verse 9: "Do not lie."
- Verse 12: "Put on . . . compassionate hearts, kindness, humility, meekness, and patience."
- Verse 15: "Let the peace of Christ rule in your hearts."
- Verse 16: "Let the word of Christ dwell in you."
- Verse 17: "Do everything in the name of the Lord Jesus, giving thanks to God the Father through him."

The whole passage is a long series of statements with imperatival force. God wants us to live a certain way. He wants us to grow progressively into the holiness we already have positionally in Christ. God wants us to move from *here*—less sanctified, less obedient—to *there*—more like Christ, more like God. And notice what he does to spur on that movement. He doesn't just give a long list of commands. He provides motivation. He offers incentives. In other words, God gives theology. If you don't care about theology, you don't care about holiness. Because what God does in chapter 3 is to give the Colossians lots of theology to stir them up to this new kind of life.

Do You Know Where You Are?

Paul says in verses 1 and 2, "If . . . you have been raised with Christ, seek the things that are above, where Christ is, seated at the right hand of God. Set your minds on things that are above, not on things that are on earth." Do you see the motivation? Set your mind on heavenly things. Why? Because you have been raised from the grave with Christ, and you have been raised in his ascension so that you now are seated in the heavenly places with Christ. Here's the logic: if, in Christ, you now reside in heaven, why are you making choices as if you lived in hell? Our present placement with Christ is a motivation for our ongoing progress in Christlikeness.

God wants to ask you a question: Do you know where you are right now? Yes, you are in your house or in front of your tablet or on a plane or wherever. But do you know *where* you are? You're seated with Christ. You're joined with him. You've been raised with him. You are where Christ is. Shouldn't this make a difference in how you live?

I remember as a child never being able to enter the dining room of our house. One whole wing of the house was quarantined for holidays and special guests. The room had white carpet with vacuum tracks always showing. There were fancy chairs and fine china. It was a sacred room. It's where we ate with missionaries or pastors, or where we had Thanksgiving dinner. There was something about being in that room. We knew as kids we were in a special place. When I sat in those tall chairs with the stiff high backs and stared at my salad and multiple forks, I knew I needed to be on my best behavior. Just because of where I was.

This is Paul's point and the engine of our motivation. If we have been raised with Christ and are seated with Christ in a place of infinite holiness, what sort of people ought we to be? Why wouldn't we live like where we live?

The You That Was and the You That Is Yet to Come

Then we see in verse 3 that we've not only been raised, but we first died. "You have died, and your life is hidden with Christ in God." To turn from your past of sin and your unrighteousness, you have to do more than just turn the page. People might tell you to turn over a new leaf, but that's not nearly drastic enough.

You have to consider your "old self" dead and buried. You have to picture Christ on the cross and see him hanging there, not only for the penalty for your sin but also for the power of sin. You have to see that on the cross with Christ is the you that was into drugs, and the you that manipulated people, and the you that was angry all the time, and the you that was filled with bitterness, and the you that lived from sensuality to sensuality. That you is dead. That's what Paul is getting at when he says, "You have died."

If we keep going on to verse 4, we see the motivation working in the opposite direction. "When Christ who is your life appears, then you will also appear with him in glory." Instead of considering what we once were in sin, now Paul directs our attention to what we will become when Christ appears and we appear with him in glory. God is reminding us, "Look, there's a better you that you'd better get used to. I'm going to make you like Christ, and that work starts right now."

Sanctification and glorification are cut from the same cloth. The latter is the heavenly completion of the former. The process of making us perfectly glorified, fit for heaven for all eternity, is underway now. God motivates us by having us think of what we will be when Christ, our life, appears. Think of who you will be without sin, without anger, without lust, without bitterness. Think of that you and live it out now.

When we want to meet a specific goal, we often visualize the completion of that goal. If you want to lose weight, for example, you get a picture of the skinny you in your mind. You hold up the picture of the muscular you you've always imagined. Whether it's a real picture or one you've made up, it's there and it's motivating. God, in a manner of speaking, wants us to visualize those spiritual jeans we are going to fit into on the last day and start squeezing into them now. "We are God's children now," the Bible says elsewhere, "and what we will be has not yet appeared; but we know that when he appears we shall be like him because we shall see him as he is" (1 John 3:2). In other words, consider what you will be and start being that person.

The Grace of Fear

We see a different kind of motivation in Colossians 3:6. Paul tells the Colossians to put away earthly desires and then says, "On account of these the wrath of God is coming." Paul is motivating them by the grace of fear.

Some people have a very hard time understanding that threats and warnings are in the Bible for our sanctification. Of course, it's wonderfully true that God will keep his elect and preserve them to the end. But how do you think he accomplishes this work of preservation? One way is by warning them of what will happen if they do not persevere. In God's people, warnings like the one in verse 6 stir us up to love and good deeds. The Christian doesn't despair at these threats of judgment. He pleads, "O Lord, keep me in the love of God as you have promised." We ought to see the warnings in Hebrews and in passages like this as God's means of preserving the saints.

Sometimes in an effort to be gospel centered, we shy away from the warnings in Scripture. I understand the impulse. We know that many tender souls need to hear how much God loves them. We need to hear about our new identity in Christ. We need to know God is for us and not against us. But there are also hard hearts in the church—maybe some reading this book—who need to know that the way they are living right now and the stuff they are into right now is why the wrath of God is coming. Some people need to be shaken from their lethargy and realize that the wrath of God will be poured out on the earth for the things they consider light and trivial offenses. Some people need the literal hell scared out of them.

But you say, "Shouldn't we be emphasizing God's grace? Isn't it all of grace? Shouldn't our preaching and counseling be all about grace?"

And, of course, it should be. But what makes us think that the warning of God's wrath is not his grace to us? We are not giving to our friends, or to ourselves, or to our people, all the grace that God has for us if we do not make known that the wrath of God is coming. God is nothing but grace to his children, but this grace can come to us in brighter and darker hues.

Speaking the Truth into Us

Paul goes on in verses 9 and 10 to describe who we are as new creations in Christ. Then in verse 11 he explains that Christ is all and in all. That's why, according to verse 12 and following, we ought to bear with one another, love one another, and maintain unity with one another. God wants us to know who we are and then live like it.

I love what these Colossian Christians are called: chosen ones, holy and beloved. Don't pass over this deliberate language. God speaks to us in this way for a reason. When I was in junior high, I played one year of football, which was one too many for me. I had kind of a gruff coach who smoked a lot and encouraged very little. The only thing I was good at was the warm-up laps. I would be way out in front of the big guys. But it didn't help all that much when we had to actually run into people during a game. Coach would sometimes say "helpful" things to me like, "Wow, DeYoung, where'd you get all them bruises?" Not quite inspirational. In high school, my cross country coach was known to say things like, "Hey, DeYoung, don't let the girls beat you." Also very encouraging.

But the best coaches know how to motivate their players, even when they need correction. He might pull you aside and say, "Look. I picked you for this team. You are as good as anyone out there. We need you in the game. Now listen, you gotta get your head in the game." That's what I picture God, through the apostle Paul, doing here in verse 12. He's gently pulling us aside to point us in the right direction.

Good parents do the same thing. The way in which a father talks to his son, and the language he uses to address him, can make all the difference. You can bark out commands to your son, or you can say, "Listen, you are my son, and I love you with all my heart. You are my special boy. You are smart and bright, and I am so proud of you. You will always be my child, and I will always be your daddy. But we got to talk about some of the things you're doing." The language of naming and identification are sincere, but they are also instrumental in motivating the child to obey. In the same way, God reminds the Colossians that he chose them, set his affection upon then, and considers them holy in Christ.

We see the same approach in the next verses. We've been forgiven, so we ought to forgive (v. 13). We are beloved, so we ought to love (v. 14). We are one body, so we ought to be at peace with one another (v. 15). You don't slap your own face. You don't kick your own shins. You don't slander the other members of the body of Christ. God speaks the truth into us that we might live according to our true God-given identity.

An Angular Gospel

Do you see the multiplicity of motivations coming from a dozen different angles? God doesn't just say, "Here's a list and do it." He says, "Let me give you the reasons to obey."

Now perhaps you hear that and think, *Okay, that's cool. I see a lot of motivations there. But, man, that's so much theology. I could never do that. I'm not Paul. I'm not a scholar. I don't think like that. When I get to talk to my children, or I got to preach a sermon, or I go to talk to my small group, I don't think of any of this. I can tell them what God commands, but I'll never come up with all these motivations.*

Well, step back and think for a moment about what Paul is doing here in Colossians 3. There are basically three prescriptions: Paul tells them what was, he tells them what is, and he tells them what will be. You died. You were raised. You're not your old self any more.

I heard an illustration one time of a pastor talking to a young man struggling with same-gender attraction. The young man called his pastor and said, "I'm feeling these things again. I'm going to go out tonight. I'm going to go to those places. I'm going to do the things I used to do." The pastor's response was extremely wise. "No, you're not going to do those things," he told him. "That's not you. That's not who you are anymore." He reminded the young man of what was.

Then we remind people of what is. You're in heaven. You're a new creation. You're in Christ. You're one body.

And finally, we need to remind each other of what will be. The wrath of God is coming. Christ is coming. A glorious appearing is coming. An inheritance is coming. You have to think of what was, what is, what will be. God uses all of it to motivate his people unto holiness.

Colossians on the Ground

We've looked at the macro level; now let's get in closer to the ground. How does God motivate us to the specific activity of holiness? In 3:18–4:1 Paul addresses six kinds of people: wives, husbands, children, fathers, slaves, and masters. We can boil down the instruction into one foundational command for each group.

- Wives, submit to your husbands.
- Husbands, love your wives.
- Children, obey your parents.
- Fathers, do not provoke your children.
- Slaves, be diligent.
- Masters, be fair.

Again, notice what we *don't* see. God doesn't give the list of commands in the way I just gave it to you. He doesn't tick off the commands like some kind of bookmark or bulletin insert. He gives reasons and provides motivation for these commands. Let's look at each of the six in turn.

Wives, Submit to Your Husbands

There are dozens of reasons wives ought to obey this command, but Paul mentions only one of those reasons here. Wives should submit to their husbands because it "is fitting in the Lord" (v. 18). There's an order in God's design, a way rulers and citizens should relate to each other, a way for parents and children to relate, a way for elders and church members, and a way for wives and husbands. It is a beautiful design. Wives shouldn't grit their teeth, swallow hard, and submit with a bitter heart because, well, "I guess it's in the Bible." God wants us to see that his design for men and women is good. It's fitting. Things work the way they should when wives are graciously, humbly, intelligently submissive to their husbands. Notice, the husband does not force submission; the wife freely gives it. God is not telling the husbands to be dictators. He's telling the wives to embrace the way God made men and women. He wants wives to do what fits.

We bought a couch from IKEA last summer. IKEA is great because the furniture is so cheap, but one of the reasons it's cheap is that it comes in big cardboard boxes. C. J. Mahaney was actually preaching at our church that weekend and was in town, so he went to IKEA with me to get the couch. Yes, it was quite a sight—the two of us walking through a maze of Swedish furniture and filling up my Suburban with cardboard boxes. Luckily for C. J., he left before I had to put the stuff together. What a pain. I opened up the four couch boxes and realized the instruction manual contained not a single word. Zero. Not in any language. All they gave me was an Allen wrench and a lot of pictures. I can't tell you how long it took me to put the couch together, but it was roughly equivalent to that of my seminary degree. I had legs pointing every which way and pieces upside down. Eventually, though, it all fit together. Just like the manual told me. Just as it was designed. Now it's a great piece of furniture.

God gives us these commands for husbands and wives so we can have a marital couch to sit on. God wants wives to submit to their husbands because this is what's right. This is his design. This is what's proper and good and fitting.

Husbands, Love Your Wives

Unlike the other five groups, no motivating factor is explicitly mentioned for the husbands. But there is an implicit appeal when Paul says, "Do not be harsh with them" (v. 19). God wants husbands to do what is good for their wives. He wants husbands to love their wives as Jesus commanded, by treating them as they would want to be treated themselves. He wants husbands to consider their wife's feelings, which was a countercultural thing to do in the first century. Some people look at these household codes and write them off as nothing but Greco-Roman patriarchy. But God's standard is actually different in important ways. A wife existed for the pleasure and the service of her husband. Considering the feelings of your wife was not the cultural norm. God says it should be. The husband must love the wife and love her in a caring, sensitive, considerate way. That's God's blueprint.

God understands the particular temptations of men and woman. In her fallenness, the wife is tempted to usurp her husband's authority, just like Eve did. So she is told to submit. The husband, in his fallenness, is tempted to abdicate his God-given headship, like Adam did, by becoming either a doormat or a dictator. So husbands are told to love their wives and not be harsh with them.

Children, Obey Your Parents

In verse 20, Paul provides a very important motivation for children to obey their parents: it pleases the Lord. Sometimes Christians can give the impression that pleasing God is a sub-biblical motivation. "We're totally justified," someone might say. "We're totally accepted. If we tell our kids to please God, we are just giving them more law. We are training them to be little moralists. We're discipling them to think of God as a kind of Santa Claus keeping a naughty-and-nice list." Obviously (or maybe not so obviously), that's not how God wants us to parent, because that's not what God is like with his children. But don't let the potential abuse of this "pleasing God" language lead you to suppress what Scripture clearly says. One of the principal motivations for holiness is the pleasure of God.

- Colossians 1:10: Those who bear fruit and every good work and increase in the knowledge of God are pleasing to God.
- Romans 12:1: Presenting your body as a living sacrifice pleases God.
- Romans 14:18: Looking out for your weaker brother pleases God.
- 1 Thessalonians 2:4: Teaching the Word in truth pleases God.
- 1 Timothy 2:3: Praying for your governing authorities pleases God.
- 1 Timothy 5:4: Supporting family members in need pleases God.
- Hebrews 13:16: Sharing with others pleases God.
- 1 John 3:22: Keeping the commandments pleases God.

Over and over, more than a dozen times in the New Testament, we have this motivation. We ought to be generous. We ought to be godly. We ought to love and live a certain way because it pleases God.

Some of us have taken justification to mean we no longer have a dynamic relationship with our heavenly Father, as if God is indifferent to our sin and our obedience. But Scripture says we can grieve the Holy Spirit, and in Hebrews 12 we see that a father disciplines those he loves. God is not pleased when we sin. Or, as John Calvin puts it, God can be "wondrously angry with his children." This doesn't mean God is ever against us as his justified people. He is always for us. But just as a parent can be upset with a child, so God can consider our actions grievous and discipline us accordingly.

If that kind of dynamism discourages you, consider the flip side. We can also *please* God with our efforts. Through the finished work of Christ, our good deeds are rendered delightful to God. When we hear the language of "pleasing God," some of us panic because we only relate to God as a judge. But he is also our Father. If you think, "I have to please God with my obedience because he is my judge," you will undermine the good news of justification by faith alone. But you ought to reason this way: "I've been acquitted. The Lord is my righteousness. I am justified fully and adopted into the family of God for all eternity. I am so eager to please my Father and live for him."

It's good to want to protect justification, but don't do it at the expense of a dynamic relationship with your heavenly Father. There is a difference between saying to your child, "God is watching over you, and when you don't share your toys, you make baby Jesus cry," and saying, "God is our Father, and when you listen to what Mommy and Daddy say and you try to do what they want you to do, it makes God really happy. He gets a smile on his face when he sees you trying to do the right thing." That's what Paul is saying here to the children at Colossae. It's how God means to motivate all of us.

Fathers, Do Not Provoke Your Children

In Colossians 3:21 Paul issues a single command for fathers, along with one reason. Do not exasperate or needlessly upset your children lest they become discouraged. Isn't it interesting that the two commands related to the men in particular have the same sort of motivation: *think of how your actions and attitude affect others*. It's as if God said, "Would you think about your wives and what it's like when you're such a harsh, boorish person? Would you think about your children when you provoke them to anger and see their countenance fall?" Paul is appealing to the welfare of those under their charge. I think he's also appealing to the natural love they have as husbands and fathers. They should *want* to make their wives and children happy.

I say with shame as a father that I have fallen on the wrong side of this command many times. I have been quick to anger. I have lost my temper and my patience. I've tried to break the will of my child and ended up crushing his spirit. God would not have us parent that way. He wants dads to think before they bark.

Servants, Be Diligent

Scripture is not promoting with these instructions the institution of chattel or race-based slavery, which we're familiar with today. The apostle Paul was simply regulating a very different kind of slavery prevalent throughout the world at the time. His instructions do not defend or advocate for the kind of institution that the word *slavery* brings to our minds. In fact, the updated version of the ESV translates *doulos* as "bondservant" instead of "slave" because the context suggests that these men and women were not treated as absolute and lifelong possessions of another. Whatever the exact situation, Paul is merely trying to address a cultural institution that showed no signs of going away.

Remarkably, the motivation is the same for both the servant and the master. In both instances, Paul says, in effect, "Remember, you have another master." He wants all those working for some mean, nasty boss to remember that ultimately they are serving God, a God who can punish and reward, a God who sees our quality. Therefore, we ought to work hard "with sincerity of heart" (v. 22). We ought to work "as for the Lord and not for men" (v. 23).

In other words, God expects us to *transpose our work into a heavenly key.* We are working for our heavenly Master, not simply our particular master. And the Master in heaven knows our hearts. He sees our efforts. He knows our trouble. It's not the master or employer down here that we need to impress, no matter what he can do to us. It's the Master up there who matters. We will stand before him on the last day and give account for our labors.

Masters, Be Fair

Paul reasons that same way for those in charge of others. He says in 4:1 that the master must treat his bondservants fairly and justly because he has his own Master in heaven. This is a good word for anyone with some degree of influence, some importance, some directional authority over others. God reminds us, "You may think you are a big shot down here, but remember there is a much bigger shot up there. And you're an-swerable to him. So treat your assistants and your employees and your junior colleagues and your interns justly and fairly." God is fair to us, so we should be fair to others. He will not show favoritism because we are important in the world's eyes. He oversees us as we oversee others. So let us exercise our authority on earth in such a way that we would be happy to be under the same kind of authority from heaven.

That's how God motivates us in the nitty-gritty of life. Can you see how all of the specific nuanced commands of God come together from above and below and behind and in front to push and to pull and to prod us to holiness? God knows what we need to hear and how we need to hear it. He speaks to us in many ways that we may make progress in the one way of Jesus.

Three Final Thoughts

What's the take-home from all this? How should this macro and micro look at Colossians 3 influence our daily walk with Christ? How should we think about the multiplicity of biblical motivations for holiness? Here are three final thoughts.

1) Don't try to be smarter than Scripture.

You may be thinking at this point: "Yes, I see many different motiva-tions. I see what you're saying, and I affirm Scripture speaks in mul-tiple ways. But if we look at the reason behind the reason, and the reasons behind that, we'll see there's really only one motivation: we don't believe the gospel. We don't know how much God loves us and how accepted we are." You may be raising that objection in your mind. And yet, as I said at the beginning, I'm suspicious of reducing all our problems to one mega problem.

I'm suspicious not because the answers don't work, but because many answers can work. I have no problem saying that at the root of every sin is some misfiring of the gospel. I think that's true. But I also think it's true that at the root of every sin is some failure to recognize the lordship of Christ, or to believe the promises of God, or to accept the goodness of God's commands, or to trust the Word of God, or to recognize our union with Christ, or to celebrate the character of God, or to find satisfaction in Jesus, or to live by the Spirit. God gives us a variety of concrete motivations, and even if in a systematic-theology sort of way we could, by logical progression, show that behind every motivation is another motivation, that still wouldn't erase the particularity of the language in Scripture itself.

Augustine was converted by reading Romans 13:12–14, where Paul says, "The day is at hand, so then let us cast off the works of darkness" (v. 12). This passage affected Augustine because it revealed to him his sin and that he could have relief from his wretched way of life. Yes, there is implicit good news in the text, but it hit Augustine with the *force* of warning and conviction of sin.

God counsels us in a hundred ways, and he exchanges a thousand truths for our lies. Let's not be hesitant to employ the full arsenal of scriptural threats and promises and examples and commands. Let's not be smarter than Scripture and say, "Well, I *see* a warning in the passage, but that doesn't seem to be gospel centered." Take Scripture; safeguard it with our theology; test it against one another. But let's understand that there is more than one way to skin a cat and more than one way to sanctify one too.

2) You need to know your people and yourself.

Wise counselors know when a spoonful of sugar helps the medicine go down and when something else is needed, like a strong tonic or a bitter pill. It takes maturity and discernment to know whether this brother or sister needs the warm hug of truth or the swift kick of truth, because truth does both. Sometimes we need the swift kick that says, "Do you not know that the unrighteous will not inherit the kingdom of God? Do not be deceived: neither the sexually immoral, nor idolaters . . . nor thieves . . . nor swindlers will inherit the kingdom of God" (1 Cor. 6:9–10). And sometimes we need the warm hug that reassures us, "There is therefore now no condemnation for those who are in Christ Jesus" (Rom. 8:1).

The Bible is always giving us reasons, always telling us why we should pursue holiness. We have to realize that by virtue of our up-bringing and our church tradition and our personality and all we're reacting against, we will gravitate toward certain kinds of motivations. When some Christians try to help people, they have only one model in mind—Jesus in the temple. So you talk to people with a curled lip and a pointed-out boney finger and feel justified in blasting them all the time. Somebody may try to say, "Hey, brother, you've got to restore people gently" (see Gal. 6:1). But all you know is that Jesus had a whip and flipped tables. And then there are other people who only think of Jesus with the little children. They figure the only way to speak to people is with a gentle, tender whisper and a warm embrace. But the language of Scripture allows us (expects us!) to approach people in different ways.

Just think of the different images for the people of God. Some-times the Bible refers to us as weak little lambs that need to be gently carried across the river. Sometimes we are a bruised reed or a smolder-ing wick. And sometimes we are cows of Bashan. If you think every-one you're talking to is a cow of Bashan, you're going to hurt a lot of people. If you think everybody is just a bruised reed and a smoldering wick, you're not going to have some of the edges you need to have when helping people. You need to know yourself, and you need to know your people.

3) Let us celebrate the all-encompassing
grace of God in our sanctification.

God has planned for your holiness. He's providing for your holiness. And he helps you grow in holiness by pulling and pushing and prodding and provoking from one little degree of glory to the next. This is all of grace—grace to call you to a holy calling, grace to empower you for a holy calling, and grace that God would condescend to try to convince you to pursue this holy calling.

Have you considered the grace of God in condescending to *persuade* us to obey? It would have been well within his right to give us a list and make his demands: "Here are the commands. I'm God, and you're not. I expect obedience. Now obey." Have you ever considered what a grace it is that the Bible is so long and has so much theology? It's God's way of condescending to our weakness to help us toward holiness. Every promise, every reminder, every threat, every warning, every propositional gospel indicative is God's grace to you. In one way, his grace has saved you, and by a thousand ways, his grace will lead you home.

3

Sinners Learning
to Act the Miracle

Restoring Broken People and the
Limits of Life in the Body

Ed Welch

It is the Spirit of Power who sanctifies us, so we would expect sanctification to feel like strength. But usually it feels like weakness—visceral, physical weakness. It felt that way for the apostle Paul, as 2 Corinthians 12 shows, and we expect that there are times it will feel that way for us.

No one likes physical weakness. It is, at least, a nuisance. At worst, it is a chronic and intrusive pain that leaves people imagining how death is better than life. But it is a frequent accompaniment to spiritual growth. When you generate a list of wise people—Joni Eareckson Tada comes to mind—most of them have been familiar with physical weakness.

It makes sense. Sanctification is for the needy, and physical disabilities certainly remind us that we are needy. Notice how much more we pray and ask for prayer when we have a physical weakness. That alone shows how the Spirit uses weakness in our sanctification. As a general rule, we expect that among God's people, the more broken the vessel, the more obvious the sanctification.

When we consider examples of physical weakness, the normal suspects come to mind: cancer, any upcoming surgeries, disabilities from accidents, headaches and other chronic pains. These and many other physical struggles are too common among us. There is another category of weakness, however, that is especially relevant in our modern era, and these weaknesses are particularly confusing and sometimes marginalized in our churches. They are the ones identified by today's psychiatry and psychiatric diagnoses.

Psychiatric diagnoses can be hard to understand, and ministry to those who have been labeled with a diagnosis tends to be either too cautious or too confident at a time when wise pastoral care is most needed. With this wise pastoral care in mind, this chapter will introduce psychiatric diagnoses, identify the basic theological tools to help those who identify themselves in psychiatric terms, and then illustrate what sanctification can look like in the midst of weakness.

Be Alert to Psychiatric Diagnoses

In only a few decades, psychiatrists have gone from being the lampooned stewards of asylums to being our great hope for emotional peace. The word on the street is that they have pharmacological answers for everything from the blitzes of mania to the weariness of boredom, and we hear rumors that new designer drugs might make us all a little better.

These hopes have led to a bifurcated world. In one, Scripture speaks about the eternal condition of our soul. In the other, psychiatry offers answers to our most pressing day-to-day struggles. Given this perceived division, psychiatry has become the *de facto* expert.

Psychiatry, of course, is not to be chastened for intruding into matters that were once the purview of Scripture. The problem is that we are unskilled at turning Scripture's gaze onto these diagnoses in such a way that Scripture continues to meaningfully interpret all things. When you hear, "I am bipolar," or "I am ADD," you hear people who feel more understood by a label than by Scripture. When Scripture seems silent on such important human experiences, self-understanding becomes secular and pastoral care suffers. A goal, therefore, is to biblically interpret psychiatric diagnoses so that those who adopt such diagnoses are meaningfully known by Scripture, wisely loved by the church community, and grow in Christ.

What Is a Psychiatric Diagnosis?

Psychiatry has gradually expanded its girth to include most things in life that are hard: the emotional lows of depression and highs of mania, addictions, fears and anxieties, disordered or chaotic thought, learning disabilities, autism and Asperger's disorder, anorexia and bulimia, cutting and self-injurious behaviors, and post-traumatic stress disorder, to name a few. Descriptions of these experiences appear in the Diagnostic and Statistical Manual (DSM-IVR) of the American Psychiatric Association (APA), and they can be found in print or on the APA website.

These descriptions aim to demarcate problems from each other and identify them rather than provide explanations. The DSM-IVR does not focus on alleged causes, and there are no clearly understood biological markers for most psychiatric problems. Those who adopt a diagnosis, however, usually assume that there are biological causes and, as a result, medicines are the premiere treatments. Given that assumption, we can understand even more why psychiatric diagnoses have become partitioned from Scripture. Scripture and pastoral care do not claim jurisdiction over medical conditions. When medical problems appear, we are content to leave them with the medical experts. As a result, sanctification becomes functionally irrelevant, and symptom relief becomes the order of the day.

Yet, even if there is a medical contribution to psychiatric diagnoses, that is not the end of Scripture's oversight or the church's oversight. The church must be *more* active when someone has a physical affliction. In the face of potentially life-dominating chronic diseases, afflicted people need a bounty of service, prayer, encouragement, and spiritual clarity. The church moves toward people who are struggling. We never simply leave them to the experts. Therefore, a rule is necessary: if someone is taking psychiatric medication, then help that person. Pastoral care should be an automatic accompaniment of medication, whether that medication is chemotherapy or Prozac.

The First Steps of Pastoral Care

A simple way to bring psychiatric diagnoses back under Scripture's purview is to move toward those who identify with a diagnosis and ask, "How can I pray for you?"

"I know that this [diagnosis and its symptoms] is probably hard for you, so you have been on my heart. How can I pray for you?"

If you are the one who identifies with a psychiatric description, ask for prayer.

This simple step is ordinary but revolutionary. With it, you break the partition between Scripture and psychiatry. Scripture is now brought close to these problems in living, and new questions suddenly appear.

How do we pray for this?

What does Scripture say is relevant?

What promises of God speak directly to the person?

Symptom relief is usually the first thought. "Pray that I wouldn't be depressed." That is a fine way to pray, but, with any problem that might be physical, we want to add, "May your inner person be renewed day by day" (see 2 Cor. 4:16).

You or the afflicted person may be tempted to think that a psychiatric diagnosis can stand in the way of sanctification. But sanctification is possible—assured even—among those who profess faith in Jesus. In fact, we expect that sanctification would be more obvious in the midst of these trials. We also expect that the basic resources we have in Scripture are sufficient for spiritual growth.

> His divine power has granted to us all things that pertain to life and godliness, through the knowledge of him who called us to his own glory and excellence, by which he has granted to us his precious and

very great promises, so that through them you may become partakers of the divine nature. (2 Pet. 1:3–4)

Remember Two Basic Theological Tools

Scripture is relatively easy to access for common struggles such as fear and anger. You simply find the dozens of relevant passages in a concordance. For the more complex and modern diagnoses of psychiatry, which rarely appear in any concordance, we need other strategies. Since at this point in church history we do not anticipate discovering a previously unearthed biblical teaching that has been overlooked by pastors and biblical scholars, we look to well-known and traditional biblical teaching for guidance. Our task is to discover new applications to old truths.

We Are Embodied Souls

The first basic truth that is crammed with potential applications is this: we are embodied souls. We are created of physical and material substance, body and soul. This is the essential and simple biblical teaching that we need. The Heidelberg Catechism begins, "That I with body and soul," in which soul overlaps with words such as spirit, mind, heart, or inner person. The Westminster Confession of Faith states, "The bodies of men, after death, return to dust, and see corruption, but their souls, which neither die nor sleep, having an immortal subsistence, immediately return to God who gave them" (32.1). There are alternatives to this position. Some believe that we are body, soul, and spirit; others that we are body alone. These alternatives are more cumbersome to apply, but they lead to similar applications.

Application, indeed, is always in view. What is it that body and soul do? How does each contribute to the whole person? Two passages send us in the right direction:

The spirit indeed is willing, but the flesh is weak. (Matt. 26:41; Mark 14:38)

Though our outer self is wasting away, our inner self is being renewed day by day. (2 Cor. 4:16)

The body is referred to as "flesh" and "outer self," the soul as "spirit" and "inner self," as well as "heart" and "mind."

The differences between body and soul can be summarized this way: the soul is the moral epicenter of the person. In our souls or hearts, we make allegiances to ourselves and our idols or to the true God. In our souls, we follow the Lord's commands or turn from them. The soul is called righteous or unrighteous, obedient or disobedient, willing or unwilling.

The body is our means of service in a physical world. It is never described in moral terms. Instead, it is either strong or weak. This means that though the body cannot make us sin, its weaknesses can make our lives complicated, difficult, and painful.

Figure 1. A graphic of the embodied soul. The heart represents the soul, the circle represents the body.

The resulting principle is critical: we can spiritually grow even when the body is weakened. More specifically, we can spiritually grow even when the *brain* is weakened or just different. Depression, bipolar disorder, and attention deficit/hyperactivity disorder (ADHD) cannot make us sin. Instead, they can be occasions for more obvious spiritual growth. This principle brings psychiatric problems back into Scripture's domain.

With this application in hand, the next task is to enlarge our understanding of physical weaknesses. When we help those who have strengths and weaknesses similar to our own, the category of the body is less prominent, and our understanding of the details of bodily weaknesses remain implicit. We know most people can read, write, remember, make plans, finish work they set out to do, and so on. We can adequately minister to them without knowing details of their strengths and weaknesses. The heart or soul is in the foreground, the body in the background. But there are times when we must understand the unique weaknesses and differences of others. Otherwise we will be impatient, without compassion, and miss Scripture that would be most relevant.

For example, if you plan to meet a friend at a local coffee shop in order to talk about a recent broken relationship, and the friend does not arrive on time, you could either get frustrated or remember that your friend is not able to drive because of poor vision and is dependent on the generosity of others to get to appointments. This would be an example of an obvious physical weakness. It is one that is easy to understand.

Strengths and weaknesses of the brain are more difficult to understand. Some people are unable to judge the passing of time. Whereas most people know that it will take at least an hour to clean a kitchen, some think they can clean it before church, even though they have to leave the house in ten minutes in order to be on time. If we ignore the biblical category of strengths and weaknesses we will assume, by default, that the tardy but well-intentioned cleaner is immoral rather than a poor judge of time. One "diagnosis" will lead to frustration and conflict; the other will encourage patience and problem solving.

Consider depression. Is it possible that someone could feel emotionally down, if not emotionally dead, and that such despondency could be an expression of brain or body weaknesses? Is it sinful to feel emotionally lifeless? There are complexities to consider here. For example, joy is commanded in the Christian life, and some might suggest that emotional deadness is in violation of that calling. Yet most Christians would agree that if someone were living with searing physical pain, we would not anticipate an exuberant display of joy. Instead, we would pray for grace in the midst of weakness, and that grace might be expressed in simply enduring pain, with few or no visible manifestations of joy, while still believing that God hears and is near.

Now add to the list. Weaknesses could include the physical experience of panic, hallucinations, disrupted sleep, poor memory, physical agitation, a mind that races from one thing to another, or an inability to make useful and practical plans.

Skillful parents are naturals at seeing their children as embodied souls. They do not excuse sin in their children, but they understand that each child has particular strengths and weaknesses, and the child who is always making a mess might be highly tactile and feels most comfortable when feeling certain textures. Such parents do not immediately identify personal inconveniences as disobedience. Instead, as careful students of children, they work to distinguish between immaturity (i.e., inability) and disobedience. With psychiatric problems, our aim is to bring these same skills to adult relationships.

We Experience Trouble and Hardship

The other theological tool needed to minister wisely and lovingly is a theology of hardships and suffering. The problems of life cluster around sin, suffering, or both. If there are brain or body weaknesses in psychiatric problems, then we need access to God's good and comforting words to those who suffer.

We also need those words for their families and friends. Imagine having a gifted and engaging son who begins withdrawing in his late teens. As he begins to shed relationships, work, and education, he becomes increasingly eccentric, then bizarre, then incomprehensible. The parents feel like they are losing their relationship with their son, they have no idea how to help, they are watching his life fall apart, and they receive solicited and unsolicited advice that often implies their culpability in what is happening. A theology of suffering will extend to both the son and the family.

The Christian church has a burgeoning cache of good books on suffering, though we still have blatant shortcomings in our ministry to sufferers, as many sufferers can attest. Among the important teachings, three stand out.

1. God has revealed himself as the compassionate one (Ex. 34:6). He is moved by the suffering of his people.
2. After the death and resurrection of Jesus, we can no longer think that our suffering is a consequence of our personal sin (unless the link is obvious). Though Job's story should have been all we needed to hear, the death and suffering of the perfect one suggests just the opposite: *the best are the ones who suffer.*
3. Suffering tends to turn us inward. Instead, the Psalms remind us that suffering is a time to speak openly from our hearts to the God who hears.

Understanding Complicated People

Equipped with these basic tools, along with a working knowledge of the doctrine of sanctification, we move toward those whose problems have been labeled in psychiatric categories and work to understand them. The simple purpose in knowing them is to encourage and help in their spiritual growth. The better we understand someone, the more appropriate and meaningful our help can be. But there is more.

With many people, knowing them helps them. To be known is helpful in itself. If you have felt misunderstood and marginalized for most of your life, and someone takes the time to know you and actually understand you, you will be blessed. Knowing and being known is a distinctive of the kingdom of heaven. It leads to unity, which is rightly prized and enjoyed by God's people. In other words, the Spirit can use the simple act of knowing someone as a means of spiritual growth. But there is more.

People have cried when the DSM initially identified them. They found relief, even something close to joy, in finally having words for their struggle. They found comfort, though the instrument was only a definition on a website. We can understand how this could happen to a person who has long been misunderstood, but we might not foresee the consequences. As a general rule, *whoever understands you best will have the most influence.* The person who cried at the definition of ADHD never cried in church but felt that she was a misfit among normal people. As such, she will still attend church, but psychiatric ways of thinking will guide her life, and psychiatric answers will gradually become her hope. The stakes in understanding people, indeed, are higher than we realize.

With this in mind, here are some complicated people we want to understand. All of them are also taking prescribed, psychiatric medications. Try to put yourself in the position of pastor or wise friend and consider what you would say as you encourage and guide them in their Christian growth.

Attention-Deficit/Hyperactivity Disorder

Do people even *have* a psychiatric disorder? Rather than thinking in terms of yes or no, it is more useful to think more or less.

Jane had more of a psychiatric disorder.

"I'll be home in an hour."

She was going to pick up some vegetables for dinner at a nearby store. Her husband usually made dinner, but she wanted to bless him and give him the night off. She was not certain what she would get, and she had not yet decided what else she would make for dinner. Just something simple. The children were grown. There was no need for anything elaborate. It was just her husband and herself.

Most people would budget about 20 minutes for the errand, but Jane knew she usually underestimated how long she took to accomplish anything, so she doubled a realistic estimate and rounded it off on the high side. That was an excellent start.

Five hours later she walked in the door, apologizing, berating herself before her husband did, sad that she had missed the impromptu dinner her husband had made and eaten, and mortified that she had done it all *again*.

She had left the house committed to a straight line—home to store and back. But she had left the house, noticed that an office supply store was having a great sale on Christmas cards, and, always wanting to be careful with money, even though it was August, she went and bought some cards. The cards reminded her that she needed to buy a birthday present for her niece's upcoming party. Since she was already out, she drove to a toy store in a neighboring town and, after much deliberation, decided on three presents. She was now two and a half hours into her trip.

With rush hour bearing down, she took a detour that pointed her farther from home but in the general direction of her close friend's house. This friend had recently shared how her life was overwhelming, so Jane stopped by to pray with her. While there, they cleaned up the kitchen until it started to get dark, when Jane suddenly realized that she needed to get home. After being ticketed for making an abrupt turn that disrupted traffic, she finally walked in the house, without the vegetables. Elapsed time: five hours, ten minutes. Ticket: $73.50.

With the exception of her husband, everyone loves Jane. She is selfless and never distracted when she is with you, as if you are the only person in the world. An indefatigable worker, she is an amazing deaconess. Everyone loves her, but they might not want to live with her, and they certainly would not hire her for anything that demands organization.

Her home is disheveled. Papers are everywhere. No one remembers the last time the dining room table was used for anything but piles.

Her husband just rolls his eyes. Between the occasional angry rants and condemning remarks, which friends and family rarely hear, he is civil but distant. Family members think he is a saint.

If we were to walk alongside Jane, the course of sanctification would begin with understanding her, which would mean seeing her through the lenses of Scripture. In some situations, ministry is straightforward.

There is sin or suffering. When there are both, as there inevitably are, we make pastoral judgments about what is most prominent. But there are other situations in which our understanding might be blurred or myopic. This is not the fault of Scripture; the shortcomings are with us.

At first, we might see Jane through the lenses of "Let what you say be simply 'Yes' or 'No'" (Matt. 5:37). Jane said one thing to her husband and did another. It is a form of lying. But lying is typically intentional, and Jane is not trying to deceive. Sadly, if the embodied soul is absent from our biblical lenses, we might not see anything else.

When considering her as embodied, we immediately become more patient, which suggests that we are on the right track.

"Jane, help me to understand what you were thinking when you left the house. These extended errands have happened before. You have left for one item and come back hours later with merchandise but not with what you planned to get."

Jane cannot even answer through her sobs.

Planning and keeping multiple tasks in mind are abilities we take for granted, unless we are very poor planners and can be easily side-tracked. Jane is wretched at linear sequencing and can be distracted to the point where she barely remembers her original plan. Her distractions are good things—saving money, praying with a friend—but they make her life chaotic.

When my own daughters were young, we had a rule that they clean their room each Saturday. On most Saturdays my wife or I would check in on them after not hearing much for a few hours, and we usually found the room in its feral state.

Why? They found a treasured toy under the mess or perhaps a good book, and they became engrossed in what they found.

Sinful? Certainly not. We gave them no deadlines for finishing their cleaning. We were usually amused by how easily they were distracted; sometimes we would help them with the job because they had difficulty knowing where to start.

With children we expect such things, but, with adults, we expect them to be just like us. If we could get to the store and back in an hour, so can everyone else. If we can clean a bedroom without stopping every minute to enjoy a rediscovered friend, so can everyone else. And we will get frustrated with those who violate our standards.

"Jane, it must be so difficult to feel like you fail at everything. With each new incident you probably feel more and more hopeless. Do you have any ideas on how I could help?"

Then Jane cries because someone understands.

Depression

Susan, married with two boys, has been depressed for twenty-three of her forty years. Depression is rarely constant, unending misery. Susan has had times when she was less depressed and times when she was more, and the fluctuations loosely followed a yearly pattern, but she is hard-pressed to identify a day that has been depression-free.

She describes depression as both internal death and massive agitation, as if she will explode if she does not escape or do something. Failure, hopelessness, and suicidal thoughts are daily companions.

She speaks at least weekly with a fine counselor who is compassionate and, as far as you know, directs her attention to Scripture and Jesus. Susan considers the counselor's help to be a lifeline. She thinks she would be dead without her. She also sees a psychiatrist and has tried most every variation of anti-depressant medication possible.

Let's say you have a friendly relationship with Susan. You know she struggles with depression, and you sometimes pray with her, but you usually leave ministry to the experts. You have become more involved recently because of an emergency call she made to the church, and the church staff alerted you to Susan's recent downturn.

"Be patient with them all" (1 Thess. 5:14). You listen and discover that she is, indeed, in extremis. Since there are others who also know her and would make decisions on hospitalization, you are free from those challenges and can focus your attention on understanding her, praying for her, and searching for encouraging words to give her.

She is agitated. She does not know what she wants or needs. When you move toward Scripture, she ignores you. When you do it again she gets frustrated.

"Can't you see what's happening? I don't want to hear the Bible!"

You ask her if you have misunderstood her pain or said anything offensive, and she calms down momentarily, but it becomes clear that she gets more agitated when you offer biblical truth.

As you try to understand her with the category of the embodied soul, you believe that depression could be a hard suffering that can appear for no apparent reason. Spurgeon said from personal experience, "You may be surrounded with all the comforts of life, and yet be in wretchedness more gloomy than death if the spirits be depressed. You may have no outward cause whatever for sorrow, and yet in the mind be dejected, the brightest sunshine will not relieve your gloom."[1] Depression can come from disordered bodies. The feeling of depression does not violate the commands of God.

Disordered bodies, however, are not powerful enough to make us indifferent or antagonistic to Scripture. Our response to God's Word is a spiritual matter. But now is not the time to press this issue with Susan. Your relationship has been stretched, and you do not want it to break. So you listen and consider deeds that might encourage her, such as simply spending time with her when she feels most vulnerable and helping her around the house. You will revisit the spiritual matters when you think she can hear them.

Panic Attacks

Steve always had a tendency toward anxiety. He preferred routines and, at forty-five and single, with the same job for twenty years, he was able

---

[1] Elizabeth R. Skoglund, *Bright Days, Dark Nights with Charles Spurgeon in Triumph over Emotional Pain* (Grand Rapids, MI: Baker, 2000), 69.

to maintain a relatively predictable life. When faced with situations in which he was unprepared or that were simply new, he would sometimes notice physical symptoms such as sweating and increased heart rate, but he would endure through them with only close friends noticing his tension.

About seven years ago, he was challenged to spiritually grapple with his anxieties rather than manage them, and he took that counsel seriously. He studied Scripture on anxiety and fear and read good books on both a biblical way of handling anxiety and general Christian growth. He shared his struggles with good friends and church elders and was quick to ask for prayer.

His growth was obvious. We all have our areas of struggle, and Steve would always have to keep an eye out for encroaching anxieties, but anxiety was instrumental in his sanctification. That's why he was shocked when he had his first panic attack.

He was out for dinner with some dear friends. The food was good and the conversation edifying. Then he noticed a visceral sensation that seemed to start in his stomach and go to his chest. Within a few seconds he felt unable to breathe. He excused himself from the table, walked out of the restaurant and leaned against a nearby tree expecting to die from either not being able to breathe or a heart attack. The episode was so intense that he started vomiting, as if his body were mobilized for nuclear attack.

By the time one of his friends came out, the episode had subsided, but he asked his friend to drive him to a nearby emergency room. The physician ran a battery of tests and identified his experience as a panic attack. He wrote Steve a prescription for an antianxiety drug, which Steve has been taking.

If you have one panic attack, you often have more. Steve began having panic attacks about once a month, almost always at times when he was relaxed—watching a movie, running an errand on the weekend, getting ready for church. He assumed this meant that he had been a failure in dealing with his anxieties. His spiritual attentiveness must have been a sham. He wondered what the Lord was trying to say to him about deep sins to which he was blind. He asks you for help.

Your first question seeks details about these assaults.

"Tell me more about your recent panic attack. Help me to understand what it is like for you and what you are thinking."

The story Steve tells could be imposed on almost all his episodes. It begins when he feels fine; sometimes he is with people and sometimes he is alone. He notices a rising discomfort, a sense of foreboding and being trapped. These give way to palpitations, which feel like his heart cannot withstand the force, and difficulty getting his breath. And his first thought is always the same.

"Jesus, help me. Rescue me."

The attack usually subsides within 5 to 10 minutes and leaves him physically exhausted.

When you ask him if there are any particular pressures in his life, he identifies work as an ongoing challenge. He has good relationships with coworkers, but the job has deadlines and little margin for error, and he feels as though it is best suited to people younger and more ambitious than him.

We could easily leave the category of the embodied soul on the shelf with Steve. Anxiety seems to be solely a spiritual matter that is clearly addressed in Scripture. So we patiently pound away with verses he has already studied. Steve is open and willing to be taught, so he will appreciate what you give him. But you would be seeing him in only one dimension if that was your approach. A theology of the embodied soul will allow you to see him more clearly, and it will point him in encouraging directions.

Consider this: is it possible that the physical manifestations of panic are, in fact, physical? They could be triggered by spiritual anxieties, but is it possible that the body, at times, can have a mind of its own? Could Steve tell his body that all is well, there is rest in Jesus, but his body does not get the message? To opt for a careful interpretation, we could say that panic attacks are at least physical. They might have spiritual contributions.

When you zero in on matters of the heart with Steve, you find sheer beauty. Perhaps the pinnacle of Christian living is, "Jesus, help." It is a resounding statement of both our need and the reigning of Jesus's strength. If we assume that sanctification looks like strength, then we will miss Steve's childlike and exemplary faith. If we look for strength in weakness, Steve becomes, along with tax collectors and the woman caught in sin, one of our heroes.

Helping Them Grow in Christ

One of the most difficult tasks in ministry is to accurately know another person. When the other person is similar to us, we can make assumptions. But the more complex the problems, the more our assumptions will miss the mark. We want to carefully understand the person, which means that we want the other person to feel understood. Then we can take the next steps of sanctification.

Attention-Deficit/Hyperactivity Disorder

"Jane, this is what I understand so far. You are an amazing servant. You love people and are quick to help. If I need someone to pray for me, you are one of the ones I would call. You bless people and are sincere in your desire to follow Jesus. But life is so hard for you, and it is hard for your husband too. Your best-laid plans are replaced by what attracts your attention at the moment. Life can feel random and chaotic."

Notice how this summary identifies both spiritual and physical realities.

"Jane, the short version is that you feel like a complete failure. Everything you do seems to go wrong. You get jobs, people love your work, then lateness and distraction get you fired, even though most of your employers hate to fire you. Now you are starting to lose hope. With each new failure, you get more depressed, and there are probably times when you believe everyone would be better off without you."

It turns out that Jane has had suicidal thoughts at times. When they come, she fights them off with faith.

Her marriage is, at best, two people living parallel lives. Her husband has withdrawn. He has had enough of her saying one thing and doing another. So you meet with them together.

He is calm and careful when you meet. He does not think anything will come of another person's getting involved. He seems to be going through the motions. He has had enough of ADHD being blamed for everything.

You try to point out two things to him. First, there are praiseworthy qualities in his wife. She does the most important things very well: she loves God and loves others. Second, her life is, indeed, very disordered and hard to understand. If he is to grow in patience, he must know her even better. To this end, you ask her if she has access to an article or book that puts words on her inner world. You ask because you wonder if they could go through such material together.

Someone else already made that suggestion, and Jane has two books ready to go. She has had two books for the past four years, but her husband has never quite found the time to read them with her, and he does not seem to be motivated now either.

The marriage is tattered. Quick fixes will be meaningless. You soon realize that faithful encouragement and prayer will be what they need most. At some point, you hope to talk about forgiveness with the husband, but at this point, the more you say, the less he hears, so you leave it for another time.

You aim for small steps. Could they agree to focus on one task? It could be getting to small group on time, laundry, or making the dining room useable. You only want them to agree.

After some discussion, they settle on the dining room. Since she has tried and failed on that job so often, you ask what might help. She immediately says, "If I had someone who could work with me—who could help me decide what to do with some of the papers and clutter—that would keep me on task." So you generate a list of names with her, and *you* call the women on the list. You fear that the process could take months if she makes the calls herself.

Two women are eager to help. So you set up a schedule for each to come once a week for a few hours. Every once in a while, the dining room table is in view, but it slowly reverts to its previous state if one of the women is unavailable.

After a few months, the marriage is essentially unchanged. Her husband has said he will read with her but has not. He seems angry, but it comes out in niceness without follow-through. (He has a profession of faith, though little involvement in church, which means you have no other appeal for help.)

So you focus on Jane, because she is eager for help, and you focus on those things that are most important. You try to distinguish between disability and sin. Her sin, of course, is the more important of the two.

She is quick to confess anger toward her husband (she acknowledges that some of her behavior is from both her distractibility *and* her anger), lack of love for being indifferent to how difficult her inconsistency has been for him, and even occasional turning away from the Lord when she blames him for her weaknesses. And her confession is with tears and a desire for the Spirit to search her heart. This is another way she blesses you in her weakness.

You try to think creatively with her. You set alarms, generate to-do lists, and place them in a place where she will actually walk into them. These and other ideas help, but they rarely initiate new habits.

Then you turn again to those things that are most important. You ask her what she is learning from Scripture, how she is loving her husband, how she is vigilant with anger, and you pray together. Her prayers are wonderful.

Meanwhile, the marriage sputters along, she is late as often as she is on time, and it might look as if little has changed. But she is, indeed, being sanctified. She is ashamed of her many weaknesses but sees them more and more as opportunities to rely on Jesus rather than on herself. She confesses her sin to her husband, even when he is distant and uninvolved. She prays without ceasing. She is finding rest in Jesus (Matt. 11:28–30). And, every once in a while, usually when she is serving someone else, you see joy.

It is not the transformation that some would like to see. It is endurance, which is arguably that most elegant expression of the Spirit's power. God is the God of perseverance, endurance, and patience (e.g., Ps. 69:7; 2 Thess. 3:5), and when we see those character qualities in other people, we are seeing the holiness of God on display.

Depression

Susan's depression is a mystery. Why has it stalked her for most of her life? What are its causes? Why has medication never really helped? With these and other questions, you have less reason to pursue her. If the experts do not have answers, you certainly will not.

New Testament ministry, however, is not dependent on in-depth knowledge of suffering and its causes. Both sin and suffering ultimately have reasons that are veiled to us, but we have all we need for sanctification even when questions remain.

The body cannot make us sin.

The body cannot separate us from Jesus and growing in him.

These can get us started.

When friends are taking psychiatric medication, we walk along with and care for them. They are saying that something is hard, and Scripture speaks clearly into those times of trials. So you continue to move toward Susan and love her wisely.

"Susan, sometimes depression seems like an invisible foe with whom it is impossible to fight. At those times, we know that God is doing something, and we probably don't have to look too hard to see it. Notice how agitation comes out when your depression is intense. Agitation is akin to frustration and anger, and those are things we can do something about. Do you remember when you got angry with me for talking about Scripture? Your depression has anger in it, and sometimes that anger pushes God away."

Depression can be so concerned with symptom relief that it misses larger spiritual realities. That is, any form of suffering is a test and trial that reveals our hearts (Deut. 8:2–3; James 1:2–4). Will Susan trust the Lord even in great distress? Will Susan endure by faith when life is hard?

> Therefore, since we are surrounded by so great a cloud of witnesses, let us also lay aside every weight, and sin which clings so closely, and let us run with endurance the race that is set before us, looking to Jesus, the founder and perfecter of our faith, who for the joy that was set before him endured the cross, despising the shame, and is seated at the right hand of the throne of God. Consider him who endured from sinners such hostility against himself, so that you may not grow weary or fainthearted. In your struggle against sin you have not yet resisted to the point of shedding your blood. (Heb. 12:1–4)

This text is rarely applied to depression, but when depression is interpreted as human suffering, which includes all types of causes, Susan is brought into Hebrews and so many other passages. Scripture is no longer silent. Her goal, along with like-minded sufferers in the history of the church, is to stand by faith. By faith Susan can hold on to the promises of God in the midst of hardship (Heb. 11:4).

As with all of us, Susan's clinging sins tend to be exposed in her suffering. We can believe that we are good Christians until suffering reveals that we are fair-weather friends. When God gives us what we want, we worship him. When he does not, we grumble, complain, and turn away, and all these reactions amount to holding God in contempt (Num. 14:11). We are essentially saying, *What have you done for me recently?*

Susan took these words to heart and confessed her sin to the Lord.

She confessed that she had stood over her Lord in judgment rather than under his love in humility. She confessed her entitlement—she thought she deserved relief. Confession is an unmistakable evidence of the work of the Spirit. Confession is power in weakness.

Susan's depression did not suddenly disappear. It continued to wax and wane in her life, still reaching crescendos at certain times of the year. But during those darker times, she would ask others for prayer and encouragement from Scripture.

This is strength in weakness. This is Susan's inner person being renewed even during hardships.

Panic Attacks

With Steve, your pastoral care is easy. You simply enjoy how he follows in the tradition of the psalmists.

> In my distress I called upon the LORD;
>   to my God I cried for help. (Ps. 18:6)

> Hear, O LORD, and be merciful to me!
>   O LORD, be my helper! (Ps. 30:10)

> God is our refuge and strength,
>   a very present help in trouble. (Ps. 46:1)

Your enjoyment will bless him. All Steve can see is his weakness, and he attributes those weaknesses to specific, yet-to-be-discovered sins. He is startled to find that his panic attacks have been occasions where he walked closely in the steps of the Suffering Servant.

He also redoubles his efforts in resting in Jesus. He chooses Matthew 11:28–30 for meditation.

> Come to me, all who labor and are heavy laden, and I will give you rest. Take my yoke upon you, and learn from me, for I am gentle and lowly in heart, and you will find rest for your souls. For my yoke is easy, and my burden is light.

His previous work in Scripture focused on trust as fear's opposite. Now he wants to learn how trust can be expressed in rest.

The most obvious change in him is how open he is with his panic attacks. Rather than being a source of shame, as they once were, they are now a way to be strengthened in weakness, and he wants others to know. In this, he continues in the tradition of the psalmists who were vocal about their hope in the Lord's power and love.

> O Israel, hope in the Lord!
>> For with the Lord there is steadfast love,
>> and with him is plentiful redemption. (Ps. 130:7)

As he was open about his own struggle, he was surprised to discover how many Christians also experienced panic attacks but were too ashamed to speak about them.

Steve has noticed that the panic attacks are now less frequent and less intense, but he mentions those things in passing. The change in his weakness is less important to him than the changes in his soul.

Acting the Miracle

We have come to expect certain things from Scripture. When confronted with complicated problems, Scripture will not minimize those complexities; it will provide insight that goes deeper than any approach that neglects its gaze, and it will respond with simple and clear direction. When considering psychiatric problems, Scripture delivers on those expectations. The primary tool that needs dusting off is teaching about the embodied soul.

The hard work is in the appropriate and skillful application of this teaching. Some parents are especially gifted at distinguishing morality and mental abilities, and they supplement those gifts with broad reading and humble questions. Some elementary school teachers intuitively understand that "bad" kids are sometimes different kids, and the differences reside in the child's strengths and weaknesses. Talented teachers understand both the moral (good and bad) and physical (strengths and weaknesses). Many of us are clumsy in these matters. All of us can grow in more skillful application.

In this chapter we have followed three different adults, each with difficult though relatively common psychiatric diagnoses, and brought them back under Scripture's domain. The result was not so much that psychiatric symptoms subsided but that sanctification became central.

The result was strength in weakness as inconspicuous saints were being prepared by their affliction for "an eternal weight of glory beyond all comparison" (2 Cor. 4:17).

4

Acting the Miracle in the Everyday

Word of God, the Means of Grace, and the Practical Pursuit of Gospel Maturity[1]

Jarvis Williams

It is my joy in this chapter to discuss both the concept of acting the miracle of sanctification in the everyday and God's means of grace that lead us to the pursuit of practical maturity in the gospel. There are three major points that I want to unpack for you by looking at selective texts from both the Old and New Testaments.

First, God's action for us and in us through Christ is the foundation underneath our pursuit of practical maturity in the gospel of Jesus Christ. John Piper set in context in his chapter the God-centered foundation underneath sanctification, and I think it might be helpful for me in this chapter to reiterate that truth briefly so that I clearly articulate that God's means of grace and our pursuit of holiness by his means of grace flow from God's great work for us and in us through Christ.

Second, God uses means of grace by which to enable us to pursue practical maturity in the gospel of Jesus Christ. I want to consider four

[1] This essay is dedicated with gratitude to Pastor Michael Caudill and Alice Caudill, Ella Prater and Willie Prater (the latter deceased since May 2012), and to Dr. Tom Schreiner and Diane Schreiner, each from whom I have learned much about sanctification in the everyday.

means of grace: (a) the Word of God, (b) preaching to yourself and meditation, (c) fervent prayer, and (d) suffering.

Third, both God's action for us and in us through Christ and his means of grace will in fact lead us to practical maturity in the gospel of Jesus Christ.

1) God's action *for us* and *in us* through Christ is the foundation underneath our pursuit of practical maturity in the gospel of Jesus Christ (Romans 8:28–30).[2]

As Piper clearly states in his chapter, God's design for our holiness began when he predestined us to be conformed into the image of Jesus. Paul supports this by stating that those whom God predestined to be conformed into Jesus's image actually experience conformity, because God's predestination of us into his image also results in our effectual calling to faith in Jesus, in our current justification before God by faith in Christ, and in our future glorification. However, in order to avoid misrepresenting the practical pursuit of sanctification, I shall reiterate the God-centered foundation of sanctification.

Paul asserts in verse 28 that "all things" work together for the good for those who love God. Then, in verses 29–30, he provides five reasons why: (1) God foreknew us (v. 29); (2) God predestined us to be conformed to the image of his Son (v. 29); (3) God effectually called us to faith in Jesus (v. 30); (4) God justifies us (v. 30), and (5) God will glorify us (v. 30). For our purposes, I'll simply unpack foreknowledge and predestination.

God's Foreknowledge (Romans 8:29)[3]

God's foreknowledge is debated. Some argue that Paul means that God's predestination is based upon the foreseen faith of those who would be-

[2] Unless otherwise indicated, all Scriptural translations are my own and from the Greek and Hebrew texts.
[3] My exegesis of Romans 8:28–30 overlaps with my new book *For Whom Did Christ Die? The Extent of the Atonement in Paul's Theology* (Milton, Keynes: Paternoster, 2012). I have used the overlapping here with permission from Paternoster.

lieve. Thus, according to this reading, God's choice to save some is based on his foresight that some would choose him. This concept of foreknowledge does occur in the New Testament in a couple of contexts where one makes a decision based on information known in advance of that decision, so that the information foreknown actually helps one to make the appropriate choice. For example, in Acts 26:5, the Pharisees foreknew Paul before he came to Jerusalem after his conversion. In 2 Peter 3:17, Peter gives his audience information about the false teachers in advance so that they can respond to them in the appropriate way with their foreknown knowledge when the false teachers seek to deceive them.

But, in my view, the above reading of foreknowledge in Romans 8:29 does not take seriously the force with which Paul discusses God's sovereignty in both the immediate and the remote context of Romans, and it does not take seriously the Old Testament roots underneath Paul's view of God's foreknowledge. When the concept of foreknowledge is applied to God and to his election of a people for his redemptive purposes, it does not refer to God's choice unto salvation based on the foreseen faith of those chosen. Rather, God's foreknowledge refers precisely to his predetermined decision to set his covenantal love upon a people for his glory. This understanding of foreknowledge is supported by texts in the Old Testament, in early Judaism, and in the New Testament. Because of limited space, a few texts from the Old and New Testaments must suffice.

Several Old Testament texts speak of God's knowledge as God's covenantal love. Genesis 18:19 states that God "knew" (chose) Abraham. In Amos 3:1, the prophet states that God "has known" (sets his covenantal love on) Israel, and Jeremiah 1:5 states that God says that before Jeremiah was in the womb, he "knew" (chose) him. Deuteronomy 7:6–7 nicely expresses what these texts mean by God's foreknowledge, even though the verb "foreknow" doesn't occur:

> The LORD did not set his love on you nor *choose* you because you were more in number than any of the peoples, for you were the fewest of

all peoples, but because the *Lord loved* you and kept the oath which he swore to your forefathers, the Lord brought you out by a mighty hand and redeemed you from the house of slavery, from the hand of Pharaoh king of Egypt. (NASB)

The most helpful examples for Paul's definition of foreknowledge are from the text of Romans. First, the immediate and remote context of 8:28–30 is strongly God-centered. That is, God's action for God's purposes is emphasized. In Romans 8:3 Paul states that *God* condemns sin. In 8:11 *God* raised Jesus from the dead, and *God* resurrects those who believe in Jesus. In 8:29 *God* calls. In 8:29 *God* predestines. In 8:30 *God* calls. In 8:30 and 33 *God* justifies. In 8:30 *God* glorifies. In 8:31 *God* is for "us." In 8:32 *God* did not spare his son but offered him for "us." In 9:11–13 *God* loved Jacob and hated Esau so that God's electing purpose would stand apart from their works. In 9:17 *God* raised up Pharaoh to destroy Pharaoh. In 9:22–24 *God* created vessels of wrath and vessels of destruction. In 9:24–25 *God* calls Jews and Gentiles to be vessels of mercy. In 11:1–24 *God* hardens some Jews so that they will not be saved and includes some Gentiles within his saving purposes. In 11:33–36 Paul praises *God* for his incomprehensible ways.

Second, Paul uses foreknowledge and predestination together (Rom. 8:30). At first, this might seem to suggest that foreknowledge and predestination are two distinct divine prerogatives in Paul's understanding of salvation. However, since Paul mentions predestination and election elsewhere in Romans (for example, Rom. 9:10–24) and in his letters (for example, Eph. 1:3–14) without mentioning foreknowledge, the two concepts (though not synonymous) are closely related, so that one implies the other. Thus Paul can speak of God's election of Jacob and Esau without using the word *foreknowledge* in Romans 9:11–12, and he can speak of his foreknowledge of Israel in Romans 11:2 without using the word *predestination*, because the two concepts are closely related.

Predestination to Conformity into the Image of Christ (Romans 8:29)
Furthermore, notice that after Paul mentions foreknowledge, he asserts that God predestined us to be "conformed into the image of Jesus Christ." The verb "to predestine" (Greek *proorizō*) in verse 29 occurs elsewhere in the New Testament, and every occurrence refers to God's predetermined choice to do something apart from anyone's foreseen faith (for example, Acts 4:28 refers to God's determining the choices of Herod, Pilate, and the Gentiles to do precisely what he wanted them to do with regard to Jesus's death; 1 Cor. 2:7 refers to God's predestination of his divine wisdom; and Eph. 1:5 and 11 refer to God's predestination of some to be saved in accordance with God's good pleasure). The term *predestine*, as Paul uses it in Romans 8:29–30, means that God chose or determined some people to be saved, for God's purposes, to be conformed into the image of God's Son, Jesus, before the foundation of the world. This interpretation is supported by Paul's statements that God predestined some humans to be conformed to the image of Jesus in verse 29, and in verse 30 that God's predestination results in the effectual calling of sinners to believe in Jesus Christ, in the justification of sinners, and in the future glorification of believers. But the major point that I want you to notice in these verses for our purposes is in verse 29, namely, that God's action of predestining some to be conformed into the image of Jesus results in their conformity into Jesus's image, and their conformity into his image is the direct result of God's foreknowledge and of his choice to predestine them.

But what is conformity into the image of Christ? It means to become like Jesus in spiritual maturity. For example, in Romans 12:1–2 Paul urges Christians not to be conformed to the present evil age but to be transformed by the renewing of their mind, and in verse 29 Paul states that God predestined some humans to be conformed into the image of his Son. Quite simply, this means that God predestined some to be conformed into the image of Jesus, which results in their lives of obedience to Jesus. To state the point another way, Paul refers in 8:29

to predestination unto salvation, which includes spiritual transformation by faith in Jesus through the power of the Spirit, and this spiritual transformation results in a changed life of obedience for all of those whom God has predestined to be conformed to the image of Jesus. I think this is one reason that Paul emphasizes ethical exhortations in Romans 12:1–15:12.

Ephesians 1:3–5

Paul emphasizes this foundational act of God elsewhere in his letters. For example, in Ephesians 1:3 Paul asserts that God has blessed us with every spiritual blessing in the heavenly places in Christ, and then he asserts in verses 4–5 that:

1. God chose us in Christ *before the foundation* of the *world to be holy and blameless* (v. 4).

2. God predestined us in love *for adoption* to be *his sons through Christ* (v. 5).

The holiness of the believer is not *optional*! Instead, it is the reason for which Paul states here that God chose us in Christ before the foundation of the world.

Ephesians 2:4–6

Ephesians 2:4–6 makes a similar point: "But God, being rich in mercy, because of his great love with which he loved us, even when we were dead in trespasses and sins, he made us alive together with Christ (by grace you have been saved), and he raised us up and he seated us in the heavenly places in Christ." And in 2:10 Paul states that those whom God made alive were in fact created in Christ Jesus to walk in good works.

2 Thessalonians 2:13

That God's action is the foundation underneath our pursuit of holiness is further evident in 2 Thessalonians 2:13:

> But we always give thanks for you, brothers, who are *loved by the
> Lord*, *because God chose you* as the first fruits *for salvation through
> sanctification by the Spirit and through belief in the truth*.

Paul's point here is that God chose us to be converted. Paul's soteriological package includes both justification and sanctification, although Paul
would distinguish between these two soteriological realities (compare
Rom. 3:21–4:25 with Rom. 6:1–23). God's sovereign election of us unto
salvation includes our sanctification. That is, it includes our holiness.

1 Peter 1:3–5

This sort of language isn't unique to Paul. Peter likewise makes the
same points about God's action in and through Jesus as the foundation
underneath our pursuit of sanctification. In 1 Peter 1:3–5 Peter praises
God for his great work of salvation:

> Blessed be the God and Father of our Lord Jesus Christ, who caused
> us to be born again according to his great mercy for a living hope
> through the resurrection from the dead to an incorruptible, unfad-
> ing, and undefiled inheritance, which is being kept in heaven for you
> who are being kept by the power of God for a salvation ready to be
> revealed in the last time.

After these remarks, Peter exhorts his audience, in 1:13–16, to be holy
since God is holy, and this exhortation basically dominates the en-
tirety of 1:13–5:10. So 1 Peter 1:3–5 asserts: praise God because he
has saved you. Then 1:13–5:10 commands believers to be holy because
God is holy.

2 Peter 1:3–11

That the foundation of holiness is God's action for us and in us through
Christ is also evident in 2 Peter 1:3–11. Here, Peter asserts that since
God's divine power has given us everything for eternal life and godli-
ness, we therefore should make every effort to add to our faith moral

excellence, knowledge, self-control, steadfastness, and godliness. But how does understanding God's foundational action underneath our pursuit of holiness practically apply? Quickly, I offer three points of practical application.

(1) God chose us or predestined us before the foundation of the world to hear the gospel, to believe the gospel, and to obey the gospel. (2) Unless God worked for us and in us through Jesus and through his Spirit, we would never have believed the gospel, and we would never desire to pursue maturity in the gospel. We would never desire holiness. (3) But since God has chosen all Christians to be in Christ, to hear the gospel, to believe the gospel, and to obey the gospel, all Christians have the moral capacity with God's help to obey the gospel by the power of the Spirit and to grow daily in sanctification and to pursue it with great intensity.

2) God uses means of grace by which to enable us to pursue practical maturity in the gospel of Jesus Christ.

I will spend the rest of this chapter discussing this truth. To reiterate my earlier points regarding God's foundational action, God predestined us to be holy. Yet he does not leave us to ourselves to pursue holiness. Instead, he predestined us to be conformed into the image of his Son; he gives us the faith to believe the gospel; he enables us to obey the gospel, and he gives us means of grace by which to obey it. There are many means of grace, but I want to focus on four that the Spirit uses to enable us to pursue maturity in the gospel.

The Word of God

First, the Word of God is a powerful means of grace that enables us to pursue maturity in the gospel. We see the power of God's word in creation in the first words of Scripture, in Genesis 1:1–3. As the rest of the narrative of Genesis 1–2 demonstrates, God created the heavens and the earth by his word.

We also see the power of God's word in that it gives physical life. When Lazarus died, Jesus (the living word of God) spoke the word of God to Lazarus's dead body when he commanded him to come forth from the tomb (John 11:43). He raised Lazarus from the dead by his powerful word (John 11:44).

The power of God's word also becomes apparent in that it gives spiritual life. In Romans 10:17 Paul says that "faith comes by hearing and hearing through the word of Christ." In Ephesians 1:13 he asserts that when the Ephesians heard "the word of truth," the gospel, they believed in Jesus.

God's word is also a powerful means of standing firm in our Lord, Jesus. According to Ephesians 6:10–17 God's word is a means by which we stand firm in Jesus and fight against the Devil. Notice that Paul mentions standing firm or withstanding four times (vv. 11, 13, 14 [stand], and v. 13 [withstand]), which I think is another way of exhorting the Ephesians to fight against the Devil in light of Paul's remarks in verse 12 that we do not wrestle ("fight") with flesh and blood. In verse 10 Paul explicitly exhorts them to fight against the Devil, when he commands them to "be strong in the Lord and in the strength of his might" (another way of saying "stand firm"), and in verse 11 when he exhorts them to put on the whole armor of God. What is the armor of God? I think it's both the gospel and the Scriptures, because Paul commands the Ephesians in verses 14–15 to stand firm by girding up their loins with truth and by putting on their feet the gospel of peace, and because in verse 17 he commands them to receive the sword of the Spirit, "which is the word of God." So I think that the gospel and the Scriptures are in fact the armor of God that Paul exhorts the Ephesians to put on.

But why does Paul command the Ephesians to be strong in the Lord Jesus and to arm themselves with the word of God in the gospel and in the Scriptures? He tells us in verses 11–12: "So that you may be able to *stand* against the wicked schemes of the devil. For our struggle is not against flesh and blood, but against the rulers, against the authorities, against the cosmic powers of this present darkness, against the spiritual forces of evil in the heavenly places." As a result of his remarks in verses 11–12, he exhorts them again in verses 13–14 to take up the whole armor of God, so that they may be able to fight against the Devil.

Paul makes clear that sanctification is a fight and that God gives us the gospel and the Scriptures as means by which he enables us to fight for sanctification and to win the battle. So let's apply this practically. (1) Read the Scriptures *regularly*. If you don't read the Word of God, you don't stand a chance of successfully fighting against the Devil, against sin, or against your flesh. (2) Be *intentional* about reading the Word of God. (3) *Pray* the Word of God for your lives. Pray through the psalms; pray through Romans, pray through Galatians; and ask the Spirit as you do so to apply the truths of God's Word to your soul. (4) Incorporate singing the Word of God into your devotional lives. (5) Memorize the content of the Scriptures. (6) Study the Scriptures. (7) Wrestle with them and chew them so that you digest them into your soul. (8) Be intentional about applying the Scriptures to your life by looking for ways to live out the text in community with other people.

Preaching to Yourself and Meditation (Psalm 42)

Second, preaching to yourself the truths of God and meditating upon the truths of God are means by which God enables us to pursue maturity in the gospel. A great example of preaching to oneself is Psalm 42.

Psalm 42 is a song of hope mingled with despair. The psalmist expresses despair in verses 1–4 and 7–10 and hope in verses 5 and 11 in the midst of despair. The psalmist preaches to himself in verses 5 and 11 and exhorts himself to hope in God. Since the psalmist's hope in God occurs in the context of his preaching to himself, one could argue that a means by which he hopes in God in the midst of his despair is by reminding himself of the God who has saved him and whom he believes will save him. Verses 5 and 11 support this.

Notice verses 5 and 11: "Why are you in despair, O my soul, and why are in turmoil within me? Hope in God, for I shall again praise him, my salvation and my God. . . . Why are you in despair, O my soul, and why are you in turmoil within me? Hope in God, for I shall again praise him, my salvation and my God."

Application: preach to yourself the gospel and the Scriptures every day. Yes, you should listen to biblical preaching on a regular basis. But you should also preach to yourself individually. When you doubt God's love for you, preach to yourself Romans 5:6–11. When you forget God's faithful provisions for you, preach to yourself verses that speak of God's faithfulness. When you are tempted to lust, preach to yourself verses that exhort you to flee from lust. When you sin, do not despair and do not give up, but preach to yourself verses that exhort you to repent of your sins and verses that talk about the forgiveness of sins found in Jesus if you repent. When you feel condemned, preach to yourself that there is no condemnation for those who are in Christ Jesus (Rom. 8:1). When you struggle with pride, preach to yourself verses that emphasize the humility of Jesus (such as Phil. 2:6–9).

If you struggle with racism, preach to yourself verses that emphasize Jesus's death for the nations (such as John 3:16 and Rev. 5:9–10). Preach to yourself verses such as Ephesians 2:11–22 that emphasize God's work of reconciling Jews and Gentiles into one new man through the cross and resurrection of Jesus Christ. Preach to yourself verses that remind you of the priority of taking the gospel to the nations (for example, Matt. 28:16–20). And then look for practical ways by which to act out those verses in reality by intentionally reaching out to others from different races and ethnicities.

If you struggle to love your enemies, fight against hate by preaching to yourself verses that remind you to love your enemies and then look for opportunities to display love to them. We should do this because God uses the Scriptures and the gospel as means by which to enable us to pursue holiness and because we so easily forget the truths of the gospel. Thus we need to remind ourselves of things that we've forgotten (for example, see 2 Peter's numerous statements about reminding God's people of what they already know).

Fervent Prayer

Third, fervent prayer is a means by which God enables us to pursue maturity in the gospel. Paul was a prayer warrior! For example, in Ephesians 1:18–19 he says: "I pray that the eyes of your heart may be enlightened, so that you will know what is the hope of your calling, what are the riches of the glory of his inheritance in the saints, and what is the surpassing greatness of his power toward us who believe." Ephesians 3:14–19 says,

> For this reason, I bow my knees before the Father, from whom every family in heaven and on earth derives its name, so that Christ may dwell in your hearts through faith and that you, being rooted and grounded in love, may be able to comprehend with all the saints what is the breadth and length and height and depth and to know the love of Christ which surpasses knowledge, that you may be filled up to all the fullness of God.

In Philippians 1:3–4 Paul says, "I thank my God in all my remembrance of you always offering prayer with joy in my every prayer for you all." In Philippians 1:9 he says, "And this I pray, that your love may abound still more and more in real knowledge and all discernment."

In Colossians 1:9 he says: "For this reason also, since the day we heard of it, we have not ceased to pray for you." In 1 Thessalonians 1:2–3 he says, "We give thanks to God always for all of you, making mention of you in our prayers." And in 1 Thessalonians 5:17 he exhorts the church to pray without ceasing.

Why this emphasis on prayer in Paul's letters? I think the answer is that Paul believed that prayer is a means by which God granted maturity in the gospel. For example, prayer is a means by which Christians understand the wisdom and revelation of God (Eph. 1:15–23; 3:14–20).

Paul prays that God would give to the Ephesians a spirit of wisdom and revelation in knowledge (Eph. 1:18), that he would enlighten the eyes of their hearts so that they would know "the hope of his calling, the riches of his glorious inheritance in the saints, and the surpassing greatness of his power in us who believe in accordance with the working of his strength" (vv. 18–19), and he states that this is the same power that God worked in Christ to raise him from the dead and to seat him at his right hand in heaven above everything (vv. 20–23). In 3:14–20, Paul prays that God would grant the Ephesians to be "strengthened with power through his Spirit in their inner being, so that Christ may dwell in [their] hearts through faith—that [they], being rooted and grounded in love, may have strength to comprehend with all the saints what is the breadth and length and height and depth, and to know the love of Christ that surpasses knowledge, and that [they] may be filled with all the fullness of God."

Prayer is a means of being strong in the Lord and overcoming the schemes of the Devil (Eph. 6:10–18, especially v. 18). In Ephesians 6:10–18 Paul urges the Ephesians to be strong in the Lord and to put on the entire armor of God (the gospel and the Scriptures) so that they would be ready to fight against the Devil and his schemes of evil, and in verses 18–19 Paul exhorts them to pray "at all times in the Spirit with all prayer and supplication" and to keep alert with all perseverance as they make supplication "for all the saints." He also asks the Ephesians in verse 19 to pray for him so that he would boldly proclaim the gospel. Thus in Ephesians 6:10–19 prayer is connected with standing firm in the Lord (v. 10), with perseverance in the faith (v. 18), and with faithful gospel proclamation (v. 19).

But what types of prayers are God's means of leading us to the pursuit of maturity in the gospel? We should pray God-centered prayers, Christ-explicit prayers, Spirit-filled prayers, and Scripture-informed prayers. The exaltation and the glory of God in Jesus Christ should be the goal of our prayers, the empowerment of the Spirit should be the nature of our prayers, and the Scriptures and the gospel should be the guides of our prayers.

If you want God to answer your prayers with regard to sanctification, pray Scripture. Pray Romans 5:6–11. Pray Psalm 42. Pray John 3:16. Pray the prayers of Paul in his letters. Pray the psalms. Pray Galatians 5:22–26. Pray that God would work the truths of the gospel in your lives and in your hearts through the power of his Spirit.

Suffering

Fourth, Paul's suffering was a means of his sanctification. In 2 Corinthians 4:1–5:21 Paul asserts that he and his fellow missionaries suffered severely for the gospel, but they did not lose heart (they did not give up), because God was using their suffering to work in them an eternal weight of glory beyond all comparison to their earthly sufferings. As a result of God's suffering, Paul delighted more strongly in the treasures of the glorious gospel of Jesus.

Furthermore, 2 Corinthians 12:7–10 supports that suffering for the gospel is a means by which God enables us to pursue maturity in the gospel. Here, Paul speaks of his thorn in the flesh. In verse 7 he states twice that God gave him this thorn to "keep him from becoming conceited because of the surpassing greatness of the revelations," of which he speaks in verses 1–6. So here Paul explicitly connects suffering for the gospel with humility, which supports that his suffering served as a means by which God kept Paul humble. God gave him this thorn (which may have been suffering for the gospel; see v. 10) to keep him from being arrogant about the revelation of Paradise (2 Cor. 12:1–6).

The New Testament also teaches that God uses the various sufferings of life as means by which he enables us to achieve maturity in the gospel. In Romans 5:3–5 Paul states that God uses any sufferings that we experience (not just suffering for the gospel) to help us mature in Christ. He says there that suffering produces "endurance, character, and hope, and hope will not disappoint." James makes the same point in James 1:2–4 when he asserts that we should rejoice when we experience various trials, because such trials will produce steadfastness in the faith, and steadfastness in the faith as a result of trials will result in blamelessness before God (maturity in the gospel).[4]

Examples of Suffering as Means of Grace

I have seen God use suffering as a means of grace to increase holiness in the lives of so many Christians throughout my brief seventeen years of being a Christian. Because of limited space, two examples must suffice. First, in 1996, when I was seventeen, my dear friend Merri-Kathryn Prater sustained a severe brain injury due to a tragic car accident. Prior to her accident, I was not a Christian. Jesus used the faith of her family and their suffering as means by which he drew me to himself in faith. When my friends and I visited Merri-Kathryn in the hospital, her mother, Ella Prater, and her father, Willie Prater (deceased since May 2012), would comfort us by pointing us to Jesus. They prayed with us, and they would invite us to sing hymns with them in the lobby of the hospital. During this experience, for the first time in my life I began to see Christianity lived out in a radiant way through the Prater family to the point that I began to desire and love their God. Consequently, a few weeks after Merri-Kathryn's death, God brought me to faith in his Son. In addition, he also strengthened Ella's and Willie's confidence in God's comprehensive sovereignty over all things, including his sovereignty over their daughter's death. Ella delights in his sovereignty with joy! Through Merri-Kathryn's death, Jesus strengthened the faith of so many saints at our church, and he used Merri-Kathryn's life and death and the faith of Ella and Willie as means by which he strengthened the church's faith, joy, and confidence in his sovereign plan.

Unfortunately, this was not the last time that my home church witnessed this sort of tragedy during my teenage years. My pastor, Michael Caudill, and his wife, Alice Caudill, suffered the death of their sixteen-year-old son. He collapsed and died at baseball practice. This devastating tragedy, of course, sent shock waves throughout our church in Hindman, Kentucky, and throughout our small community. But God used this tragedy as a means by which he deepened the love, joy, and faith of Pastor Caudill and Alice. Their love for Jesus was great before their son died, but their love for Jesus and his gospel is even greater now, because God used this tragedy as a means by which he strengthened their joy, faith, and hope in Christ.

Here's the application: when you suffer, of course, ask Jesus to take it from you, but also ask him to use it to keep you in the gospel and to serve as a means by which he will enable you to pursue conformity into his image.

3) God's action *for us* and *in us* through Christ and the means of grace that he gives to us will *in fact* lead us to achieve practical maturity in the gospel of Jesus Christ.

Because of God's work in us, Christians will experience spiritual progress with God's help. Some Christians may experience rapid progress, and others may experience slow progress in maturity. But Christians *can* and in fact *will* experience maturity in the gospel, because God has worked in us through his Spirit to achieve this end.

Maturity in the Gospel Is God's Will for Christians
Paul states in 1 Thessalonians 4:3–8:

> This is the will of God: your sanctification: that you abstain from sexual immorality, that each of you know how to control his own vessel in holiness and honor, not in the passion of lust like Gentiles who do not know God, that no one transgress and wrong his brother in this matter, because the Lord is an avenger in all these things, as we told you beforehand and solemnly warned you, for God has not called us for impurity, but in holiness. Therefore, whoever disregards this, disregards no man, but God, who gives his Holy Spirit to you. (NRSV)

In Galatians 5:16–26 Paul warns the Galatians not to practice the lusts of the flesh or else they will fall short of inheriting the kingdom of God. But he urges them to practice the fruit of the Spirit,[5] which gives the impression that they can walk in the power of the Spirit with the help of the Spirit.

Actively and Aggressively

Because of God's work for us and in us through Christ and because of God's means of grace, Christians should pursue practical maturity in Christ with great intensity by fighting against the Devil and the flesh. As Paul states in Philippians 2:12–13, we should "work out our salvation with fear and trembling because God is the one who has worked in us both to will and to work for his good pleasure." Christian obedience is *God's "work" first and it's our work too, because of God's work in us.* His sovereign work in us does *not* cancel our need to work out our salvation or to pursue him with great intensity. Instead, his work in us propels us to do so; that is, we should wear ourselves out intensely pursuing God through various spiritual disciplines and means of grace because he has worked in us.

We should not passively sit back and allow the Devil and the flesh to defeat us or to strip us of the freedom, the joy, or the victory that we have in the gospel. But we should actively and aggressively use the spiritual resources and means that God has given to us so that we can both pursue and experience maturity in the gospel. Christians should not live a defeatist lifestyle. We can overcome the sins of racism, sexual immorality, lust, and more with God's help because of his work in us and for us through Christ as we rely totally on him and as we use his means of grace by which to do so. With God's help and by his grace, we can act out the miracle of sanctification in the everyday!

---

[5] See also the number of texts in Ephesians 4:1–6:9 where Paul exhorts Christians to pursue obedience in the gospel. See also 2 Peter 1:3–11.

Acting the
Miracle Together

Corporate Dynamics in Christian Sanctification

Russell Moore

If you see something, say something. That's what you'll see on signs everywhere in and around New York City subway stations. These signs are part of a public relations campaign meant to encourage citizens to be on the watch for potential terrorists. If a member of the public observes something suspicious, he or she is encouraged to notify the authorities. This way, so the logic goes, the city of New York will be better equipped to deal with potential terrorists. Since its inception, there's only been one problem with this campaign.

It doesn't work.

Not a single terrorist has been caught as a result of this campaign. Why? Well, as one article put it, there's just too much weird stuff going on in New York. "We have everything," says sociologist Harvey Molotch. "People lugging their art project around with wires sticking out, people who indeed look Islamic operating machines to count their prayers in Islam as they go."[1] All around the New York City subways are people who seem suspicious and out of place, but they aren't; they're just part of the bizarre and eclectic group of peo-

---

[1] Dwyer Gunn, "Does 'See Something, Say Something' Do Nothing?" *New York Magazine*, October 1, 2012, 10.

ple that make their home in New York. The problem, then, is that no one can call in and report suspicious activity because they don't know what qualifies as suspicious. They don't know what normal is supposed to look like.

Not Knowing What's Normal

That's not only true on the subway in New York City. Part of the obstacle that those of us in Christ face when it comes to growing in holiness is that we ourselves don't know what normal looks like. We've lived our entire existence in a fallen universe, as Isaiah tells us, "in the midst of a people of unclean lips" (Isa. 6:5), even as we ourselves are people of unclean lips. And in the midst of all the fallenness around us, what seems to be perfectly normal can, in fact, be sinful. What seems to be perfectly normal, and in some cases even respectable, can be completely overlooked for the sin that it is, simply because one is living around so many other people who have similar sorts of slaveries and bondage to sin such that it doesn't even seem abnormal.

What the gospel of Jesus Christ does, though, is break through this bizarre, unnatural kind of life we are living and puts forward a new normal that Jesus defines as the kingdom of God. And this kingdom, Jesus tells his apostles, isn't just some generic category referring to God's power, and it isn't some place we await for another thousand or trillion years. This kingdom shows up in assemblies—and it shows up now.

Where We See the Reign of Christ

At Caesarea Philippi, Jesus speaks of the coming of the kingdom, about its advance. "The gates of hell shall not prevail against it," Jesus says (Matt. 16:18). The power of Satan will not overcome this kingdom. Not only that, but Jesus shows that the reality of his kingdom will be seen in the fact that he will build it; Jesus will assemble his people together. For there is no kingdom, the Bible tells us, where there is no people. There is no reign where there is no empire over which to reign. Where, though, do we see this kingdom, this assembly of people over which Jesus reigns? We see these people, and this reign, in one place—the church.

The visible sign that Jesus gives in the church, therefore, is a sign of the manifold wisdom of God, a sign to the principalities and powers in the heavenly places where God has appointed Jesus to rule over his church as a head to a body, as a king over a kingdom. While the whole world indeed "lies under the sway of the wicked one" (1 John 5:19 NKJV), and while there yet remains an evil "god of this age" (John 12:31; 2 Cor. 4:4), in the local assemblies of the church, we see a sign of the reign of Christ.

Sanctification as Corporate

One problem we have today when it comes to the issue of holiness is that we think of sanctification as primarily an individual thing. We ask ourselves, "How often am I reading the Bible and praying? How often am I singing praise to God and meditating upon the things of God?" And while all of these are indeed important, too often we neglect the fact that we are holy and grow in holiness only because we are part of the body of Christ—in a real and vital union with Christ in the body he has knit together. The question of sanctification, then, is not, what are *you* doing to promote your growth in godliness, but what are *we* doing.

That's why Paul's letter to the Corinthian church is so significant. He is writing to a group of people living at the very earliest stages of the new reality Jesus promised at Caesarea Philippi—the building and gathering of his church. And this gathering has significance not just for the first-century church in Corinth but also for us and our sanctification. First Corinthians 4–6 is particularly helpful in highlighting this corporate nature of sanctification, and below we'll see a number of different ways the kingdom of Christ leads us to act the miracle of sanctification *together*.

1) Sanctification and the Church's Proclamation

Paul writes to a church in Corinth that is troubled and filled with arrogance, with those who act as if they are already kings (1 Cor. 4:8). Paul, by contrast, has lived his own life as an example to them as the "last of all," a "spectacle to the world," and a "[fool] for Christ's sake" (vv. 9–10). Paul has given them the gospel and exists as their spiritual father (v. 15); he has sent Timothy to remind them of Paul's instructions, and he has urged the Corinthians to imitate Paul in his other-directedness for the sake of the gospel (vv. 16–17). And yet they rebel—grasping after power, and prominence, and authority, rejecting the one who is himself the reason they received the gospel in the first place. Paul, therefore, decides that he will go himself to this Corinthian church, to see these arrogant ones and discern whether what they are saying is just talk—"for the kingdom," Paul declares, "does not consist in talk but in power" (v. 20).

On first blush, such a statement from Paul reads like he's challenging the Corinthians to a fight. But instead, Paul reveals his arsenal in advance, and his choice may surprise some. Paul tells the Corinthians he will come to them armed—with words. Paul will come to the Corinthians with words bearing a spirit of gentleness and loving discipline, but unlike the empty, meaningless words of the arrogant ones, his words carry the power of the kingdom.

The Power of the Kingdom

What exactly is this power? It is the proclamation Paul brings bearing the authority and the spirit of Christ. It is precisely what Jesus means when he says, "Where two or three are gathered in my name, there I am among them" (Matt. 18:20). When the church gathers in Jesus's name, and in Jesus's power, his Spirit is there among them. Accordingly, as the Corinthian church hears the inspired words of the Spirit in the book of 1 Corinthians, there is a power that comes with these words. We see this power at Caesarea Philippi—Jesus asks his disciples, "Who do people say that the Son of Man is?" (Matt. 16:13).

On first reading, this seems to be a nonthreatening question; the disciples can just answer back with the array of opinions people have: "Some say John the Baptist, others say Elijah, and others Jeremiah or one of the prophets" (v. 14). But when Jesus asks Simon Peter, directly, "But who do you say I am?" (v. 15), he replies by the power of the Spirit, declaring, "You are the Christ, the Son of the living God" (v. 16). And then, crucially, Jesus expresses power and authority—by renaming Simon Peter.

Jesus Speaks with Authority

I don't know about you, but I've never been quite so audacious as to give someone a new name, as if I had the authority, upon meeting a stranger, say, in the hardware store, to say, "You know, you say your name is Frank, but you look like a Bob to me. Your new name is Bob." In the same way, there's a certain audacity here seen in Jesus's declaring, "I tell you, you are Peter, and on this rock I will build my church" (v. 18). Jesus's declaration seems so unreal, beyond that, because it doesn't seem to be true at all.

How does Jesus call Peter a rock, when, just a few verses down, he will rebuke him and call him Satan (v. 23)? How does Jesus call Peter a rock when he knows that it is Peter who continually says all sorts of outlandish things at inappropriate times, when he knows that it is Peter who will abandon Jesus upon his arrest? Even still, Jesus insists that Peter himself will be the foundation stone of his church. Why does Jesus say this? He gives Peter this name; he calls him a rock, because Jesus speaks with authority—and his word makes Peter live up to his name. The voice of Jesus gives to Peter a name that seems as ridiculous as an elderly barren man named "father of many nations," but Jesus makes these names true by the power of his transforming word.

Representative Authority

In the same way, Paul assumes that the apostolic authority he himself carries means that the proclamation of the Spirit-inspired words brings with it the authority of Jesus himself. Paul stands in the place of Christ and brings words with the authority of Christ.

I'm often reminded of the importance of representative authority when I'm around my relatives. Every once in a while I'll be sitting around with extended family at some holiday or event, and the news will be playing in the background. All of a sudden, I'll hear an elderly aunt or distant cousin react to something he sees on the news: "You know what we need to do? We need to bomb Canada! Who knows what they're going to do!"

Now, when I hear that, I don't argue. The particular conspiracy theory doesn't really matter. Presumably, it wouldn't even matter that much if one of my relatives traveled to the doorstep of the United Nations and stood at the doorway with a bullhorn chanting, "Let's bomb Canada! Let's bomb Canada!" People would just think it was a crazy person and go about their business.

But imagine if this relative of mine was the US Ambassador to the Untied Nations. If *that* person says, "Let's bomb Canada," then it creates mayhem. Why is that? It's because the US Ambassador is not speaking on his or her own authority but is coming with the authority of a powerful country that is able to carry out its threats.

Authority in Preaching God's Word

The same thing is happening with the authority of the preached Word of God. When you and I gather together and hear God's Word faithfully preached, what we are hearing is an ambassadorial plea that has been sent down from our Lord Jesus himself, such that Paul speaks of preaching as a ministry of reconciliation in which "we are ambassadors for Christ, God making his appeal through us" (2 Cor. 5:20). The Word of God preached faithfully, therefore, has a northern Galilean accent; people hearing such a proclamation ought to hear a familiar voice—the same one that first called them out of darkness.

Not only that, but whenever we see Jesus begin to speak in Scripture, we see things start happening. Demons start shrinking as they see their power broken. Men and women are healed at the power of the spoken words of Jesus. The same thing happens when you and I as believers gather to hear his Word preached, or admonish and teach one another and sing to one another with psalms, hymns, and spiritual songs. The ministry of the Word is not just an informational download—the proclamation of the Word of God is expository exorcism.

Written to the Entire Church

You see, the power of Jesus's voice residing in his church under the authority of the proclaimed Word of God breaks through the patterns of destruction that keep us from seeing the glory of the light of God reflected in the face of Christ. When we proclaim the Scripture, whether in sermon, song, or counsel, and when we do so not on the basis of our own authority but on the basis of the Scriptures, there is power—wonder-working pow'r—in the proclamation that creates and brings into existence exactly what Jesus says.

This is precisely why the Bible is written to the entire church and not arranged systematically according to needs for people in particular life situations. That's why, sometimes, you'll hear from that single woman, who has never been and feels no calling to be married, balk at a sermon on Ephesians 5, wondering why she has to listen to another sermon on marriage. But the reason why she needs to listen to this sermon is that Ephesians 5 isn't meant to be received only by married couples at the church in Ephesus. The passage is addressed to the entire church because the single women in that congregation, and in our own congregations, are not only accountable for their own lives but are also called to teach and hold accountable those marriages within the church.

Why does an eighty-eight-year-old man need to hear a sermon series on parenting? Because he is held accountable to teach and encourage and rebuke the rest of those within the church when it comes to parenting. You and I form a kingdom of priests under the proclamation of God's Word—a Word that creates and brings about sanctification and holiness.

2) Sanctification and the Church's Discipline

Immediately after Paul speaks of the power behind his words, and the lack of power behind the words of the arrogant ones, he changes the topic to address a scandal: "It is actually reported that there is sexual immorality among you, and of a kind that is not tolerated even among pagans" (1 Cor. 5:1). In so doing, Paul connects the authority and power of the kingdom to the responsibility for discipline within the kingdom, echoing Jesus's declaration that he has given the church the "keys of the kingdom" (Matt. 16:19).

In speaking of discipline, what naturally comes to mind for many is church discipline. And one of the problems in addressing church discipline to a typical evangelical audience is that what many of our minds immediately jump to when we hear "church discipline" is excommunication. We think that someone under church discipline is someone who has been voted out of the fellowship of the church—and in many cases, that is perfectly true. And yet, in reality, we are all under church discipline—because discipline is much more than excommunication. In fact, excommunication is the *end* of church discipline, the final phase when the church hands the sinner over to Satan, removing him from fellowship for lack of repentance.

At every step, discipline is designed to discern who is and isn't qualified to be called "brother" and "sister" within the church. Thus, when Paul asserts, "there is sexual immorality among you" (1 Cor. 5:1), the "you" he speaks of is the church—the church at Corinth that has been called out and sanctified by the Spirit and the blood of Christ. The responsibility given to this church by Jesus—dependent on and deriving from the Word of God—is to mark out and identify those who are qualified to be counted as brothers based upon the criteria of repentance toward God and faith in the Lord Jesus Christ.

Marking Out Boundaries in Baptism

Thus, in baptism, the church is marking out its boundaries; the church receives one into the baptismal waters and then into its membership upon a profession of faith and repentance and hence receives this one into its structure of accountability before God. Unlike the world, with its chaotic anarchy and satanic rule, the church is the location within the present order where Jesus rules as king, as head over a body. In baptism, then, the church—on the basis of what Jesus has said to us in the Scripture—is declaring the one going into and coming out of the water to be a brother, to be one who has been received by Christ.

No pastor or elder or minister has the personal authority to make this declaration or define these boundaries. Instead, the King of the kingdom has defined the boundaries by which one is or is not received by God. When the church recognizes those within these boundaries and speaks rightly, on the basis of what Jesus has given the church, it is declaring in the voice of Jesus, "You are one of the brothers." That is a powerful, awe-inspiring responsibility.

A More Important Vote

I'm reminded of the significance of this responsibility every four years during US presidential elections. As I flip through the channels I hear all kinds of conspiracy theories, talking heads fretful or angry about the prospect of the candidate they oppose being elected president, and, without fail, I'll hear over and over again: "This is the most important election that has happened in our lifetime." Amazingly, every election in which I've ever participated has been "the most important election of our lifetime," apparently. Now, there should be no doubt—a presidential election is of great significance. Even still, your vote on receiving a new member into your congregation is far more significant in the long term than is your vote for who will be the next president of the United States. When a congregation receives one into the baptismal waters or onto their membership rolls, they are making a proclamation that has eternal significance.

Conversely, when the congregation refuses to deal with an issue wherein there is a lack of repentance, the congregation—charged with the task of speaking on behalf of the Lord Jesus Christ—is making a false proclamation in its silence, giving the false impression that Jesus sanctions or is unconcerned with unrepentant sin.

Responsible to Speak Faithfully

The mandate for the church to discipline its members is a call to obey what Scripture has clearly commanded. It's easy, I find, to condemn the empty-suit preacher being interviewed on CNN who balks at the question, "What about well-intentioned Muslims and Hindus? Do they go to hell?" because we find the reluctance to affirm what Scripture so clearly teaches about the way of salvation to be pathetic and cowardly. And yet many of our churches fail at precisely the same point when it comes to discipline.

When we list someone on a membership roll who is continuing in unrepentant sin, or living a life devoid of faith, or refusing to gather with the assembly of the church, we are saying to them, in effect, "Jesus says that you are our brother," when we actually have no warrant to say that. We might as well go door-to-door and say to everyone who answers, "I'll see you in heaven." The church has the authority to speak—but also the responsibility to speak faithfully. And the church's proclamation comes not only from what is said from the pulpit. Even the membership of the church, we've seen, is itself a proclamation coming with the ambassadorial authority of Jesus—thus the church is called to faithfulness in its proclamation, and diligence in its discipline.

The Goal of Excommunication

All this being said, the church has authority to discipline only where Jesus himself has given that authority—in his Word. The church doesn't discipline and disfellowship someone because they disagree, for instance, over the issue of whether their children should be in homeschool or public school, or whether it's appropriate to celebrate Halloween. Instead, the church disciplines those things about which the Scripture says that those who practice them "will not inherit the kingdom of God" (1 Cor. 6:9–10; Gal. 5:21). We discipline clear signs of rebellion and disobedience and refusal to turn away from sin and live in obedience to Christ.

And when that final stage of discipline comes, when one is put out of the fellowship, we need to be clear on what that entails. Church discipline is not just "clearing the membership roll" as if the point were primarily accuracy in bookkeeping. Neither is church discipline designed to be a punishment, as if the church were saying, "We don't want your kind around here." Yes, the church speaks of this stage of discipline as the delivering of one to Satan (1 Cor. 5:5), but the very next phrase in the same verse reveals that such is done precisely for the purpose that "his spirit may be saved in the day of the Lord." Thus, the goal in church discipline is that the one being put out of fellowship will hear the warning in the church's action as Jesus's own voice, saying to him, "I am handing you over to Satan," and in response turn back in repentance and faith. If that happens, Scripture tells us, we will have "gained [a] brother" (Matt. 18:15). The church disciplines in the hope that the one being disciplined will hear Jesus's warning voice and return—as Jesus says of his flock, "My sheep hear my voice, and I know them, and they follow me" (John 10:27).

The only difference, then, between Peter's weeping in repentance in the arms of Jesus, and Judas tangled up in his own intestines in a potter's field, is the kind of repentance the voice of Jesus brings. The discipline of the congregation spurs us to holiness not only in bringing to light issues of rebellion and unrepentance, and not only because the ambassadorial proclamation from Jesus works in our hearts to bring about repentance, but also because the accountability within the church itself changes us.

Reorienting Our Lives and Affections

Notice what Paul says: "I wrote to you in my letter not to associate with sexually immoral people—not at all meaning the sexually immoral of this world. . . . I am writing to you not to associate with anyone who bears the name of brother if he is guilty" (1 Cor. 5:9–11). Paul is not trying to set up some sort of rapture in advance, wherein the church hermetically seals itself off from the rest of the outside world. That's why Paul asks, "What have I to do with judging outsiders?" (v. 12). Instead, he's demanding that the church not associate with evil *within* the accountability of the church itself.

At this point is where we tend to get things completely reversed. All too often, we express our outrage at everything going on "out there" in the world and all the while ignore the wickedness in our own midst. And yet the discipline of the church is designed to reorient our lives and affections. The discipline of the church changes our mission, because it changes the way we see people—having empathy instead of judgment on those outside of Christ, knowing they are enslaved by sin and that God himself will judge them; and at the same time being diligent in spurring on toward obedience those who bear the name of brother, knowing that the church is called to love one another and form one another with the Word of truth. In the end, the discipline of the church drives us toward love, because the presence of Jesus is in our midst by his Word and Spirit.

3) Sanctification and the Church's Economy

Beyond the proclamation and the discipline of the church, the church's ordering and structure, what is formally called the "economy" of the church, is designed to conform us more into the image of Christ. In the very next chapter of 1 Corinthians, Paul rebukes the church because they are not only tolerating immorality within their midst, but they are also fighting and struggling with one another—some going so far as to take one another to court (1 Cor. 6:1–8). Such ought to be humiliating, Paul argues, because "the saints will judge the world" (v. 2), and here are these believers laying down their disputes "before those who have no standing in the church" (v. 4). You see, the gifts Jesus gives the church are not simply designed for personal edification. Jesus gives gifts to the church for the expressed purpose of building up the body (Eph. 4:12) and for use in spiritual warfare—to show that Jesus has taken captivity captive.

We know the significance of this warfare and of taking the enemy captive. We understand when we see a picture of a US soldier standing in Saddam Hussein's bathtub that this picture is a celebration, an indication of successful conquest because the enemy is gone and our army has won. At the same time, Jesus gifts his church as preparation; in giving gifts to his church now he is staffing up his church for a future kingdom that is to come. That's why much of our focus when it comes to spiritual gifts is off target. So many of us obsess about what *our* gift is, and we take all sorts of "gift inventories" to try to figure that out. But what the Scripture reveals to us is that your gift is not "your" gift—it is given to the church for the purpose of the upbuilding of the body. So the question is not "What is my gift?" but rather "Is my gift, am I myself, operative and functioning within and for the building up of the body?"

In this light we can understand why Paul asks, "Can it be that there is no one among you wise enough to settle a dispute between the brothers?" (1 Cor. 6:5). Instead, these in the Corinthian church are taking their disputes to the outside world. For you and me, while the outside world can be a public court of law, it can just as easily be a gossip-laden court of public opinion on the Internet or in hushed conversations. In every situation, such rebellion acts as if Jesus was not victorious, as if he did not gift his church with all it needed to promote peace and godliness. In the end, these disputes make it seem like the gospel isn't true.

An Internship for the Eschaton

Not only that, but Jesus gives gifts to his church because he is training those of us in Christ now in little things, for large areas of responsibility over which we will have authority in the age to come. Our life within the body of Christ now is an internship for the eschaton. The disputes within the Corinthian church, then, are remarkably shortsighted. If you really believe the gospel, that Jesus will return and usher in an eternal kingdom, then you believe that your life now entails long-range planning—as in plotting out your next trillion years. And yet so often we get caught up in disputes; we worry about accomplishing our little agendas, maintaining our little pockets of authority, as if there was nothing beyond our own sphere of influence, nothing beyond our present life.

Imagine a kindergarten child coming home and telling his parents that he won the presidency of his kindergarten class. His parents would be excited, of course. They'd probably decorate a cake, and take some pictures, and celebrate. But if that same child grows up to be fifty years old and is still glorying in the fact that he was elected president of Mrs. Timsley's kindergarten class, that guy is, well, a loser.

In just the same way, Paul tells the Corinthian church—and us—that we are going to judge angels and rule with Christ over the universe (1 Cor. 6:2–3). And when the disputants in the Corinthian church go out and tell the outside world that the church needs help to discern what is just and good, they are declaring their own shortsightedness, and they are declaring the incompetence of Jesus to rule over his kingdom within the church.

That is why Paul rebukes the Corinthians, asking, "Why not rather suffer wrong? Why not rather be defrauded?" (1 Cor. 6:7). In light of the mission the church has received, in light of the big picture and the glorious future in store for those in Christ, what real significance does your dispute, your problem, your preference have? Who cares?

The Outward Direction of Corporate Worship

So often we see these kinds of disputes in our midst when it comes to music. Now, I myself have the worship taste of a seventy-five-year-old woman. I feel most at home with Fanny Crosby, hearing "Victory in

Jesus" and "Brethren, We Have Met to Worship," even more if it's set to fiddle. What I had to learn, though, no matter what the old hymn says, is that when it comes to worship, I don't "come to the garden alone."

In a real sense, our worship wars are of one piece with these disputes going on in the Corinthian church. We act as if worship is designed to provide the individual with whatever it takes for him to close his eyes and pretend that he's having a moment with Jesus, enjoying a little foretaste of heaven. The problem, though, is music is not given to the church primarily so you can have a moment with Jesus. In Scripture, we see that we are given song to build one another up in faith, to do warfare with one another against the principalities and powers in the heavenly places, and to prepare one another through worship for a new era and a new creation. Worship in Scripture, then, is outward-directed, whether directed toward warfare, one another, or the age to come. We have then, it seems, the wrong kind of worship wars. There should be disputes about our music, but if we have a biblical understanding of worship, and of sanctification, then our disputes will consist of the elderly woman concerned that there are too many old hymns being played and not enough Lecrae, and twenty-somethings in the college ministry demanding that the church turn down the volume a little and play some "more familiar" songs in worship—each concerned for the others' well being and edification. Those within the church are called to count others as more important than themselves, outdoing themselves in showing honor to one another (Rom. 12:10). For in worship, and in service with one another within the life of the body, you and I are being shaped and prepared for something that is far deeper and wider and more important than your favorite worship style. We're being prepared to rule.

4) Sanctification and the Church's Testimony

In a recent op-ed, columnist David Brooks argued that we live in an arena culture.[2] By that he means that the things that tend to give peo-

---

[2] David Brooks, "The Arena Culture," *New York Times*, December 31, 2010, A23.

ple meaning in today's culture take place in arenas, like politics and sports. You see this all over the place; people identify with their team, or party, or candidate, such that for many, when you speak a word against "my candidate," or "my team," it feels as if you're speaking a word against *me*.

On the other hand, there is an appeal to this arena culture because it provides a sense of community. You find yourself in an arena full of people with the same goal, the same shared interest; in turn this shared goal—whether it's beating the Yankees, or beating the Democrats, or whoever else—provides a larger metanarrative, makes it feel like your life transcends its own little meaning, and is a part of something bigger.

And yet the arena that God calls us to in our sanctification is set on a stage much bigger than any stadium or convention site. The backdrop of this arena is eternity. That's why Paul is imploring the Corinthians, "Do not be deceived" (1 Cor. 6:9), and continually reminding them of those who will not inherit the kingdom of God (1 Cor. 6:9–10; 15:50; Gal. 5:21; Eph. 5:5). In the arena in which we find ourselves, the stakes are high. But the power of Christ in the life of the church breaks through the deception of the satanic powers.

The Power of Community in the Process of Sanctification

The power of the community in the process of sanctification is seen in the way that it's easy for many of us to identify the sins of others but justify or be blinded to our own. That's why Paul is listing off these sins the Corinthians are guilty of—"neither the sexually immoral, nor idolaters, nor adulterers, nor men who practice homosexuality, nor thieves, nor the greedy, nor drunkards, nor revilers, nor swindlers will inherit the kingdom of God" (1 Cor. 6:9–10). In calling out these brothers he is warning them, revealing the way in which they are in their sin believing the same lie as did the primeval couple: "You will not surely die" (Gen. 3:4). The word of the church breaks the power of the deception of sin.

Beyond that, the word of the church breaks the power of Satan's accusation. Notice Paul's crucial distinction. He is *not* saying that sexually immoral people do not inherit the kingdom but regular people do. He *is* saying that sexually immoral people do not inherit the kingdom, but sexually immoral people *who crucify their sin* do inherit the kingdom. That is precisely the point of hope in Paul's message to the Corinthian church; the sexually immoral and the greedy will not inherit the kingdom, "and such were some of you. *But you were washed, you were sanctified*, you were justified in the name of the Lord Jesus Christ and by the Spirit of God" (1 Cor. 6:11).

Speaking to Others—and to Ourselves

You see, being together in the fellowship of the church and learning to bear with one another's sins and point out one another's blind spots, points us to the reality of our own standing before God—not as some neutral "regular" person, but as a sinner who deserves to hear, "I never knew you; depart from me, you workers of lawlessness" (Matt. 7:23). The truth of the gospel is that, though "such were some of you," the blood of Jesus cleanses you from sin.

So when a congregation receives into membership the man who says, "I broke up my family; I abandoned my children, and I am haunted every day by their screams when I walked out the door," and speaks to that repentant soul with the authority of the risen Jesus saying, "Your sins have been forgiven you," we are speaking also right back to ourselves. The same blood that cleanses the swindler cleanses the idolater. The same blood that cleanses the fornicator cleanses the thief and the self-righteous legalist. Why? Because the gathering of the church together is a sign to the principalities and powers not that the assembly is a group of sinless people but is instead a group of people who will no longer bear accusation—because the reign of Jesus through his crucifixion and resurrection of the dead cancels the power of Satan's accusations.

Guilty—but Forgiven

Because this is the case, when the woman in our congregation cries when she hears the words of a certain hymn because she remembers having an abortion, what we say to her is not, "It's okay." Neither do we say, "Actually, those who practice bloodshed *will* inherit the kingdom of God." Instead, we teach her that if she is in Christ, she can sing out these songs, and sing right at the Devil, saying, "You are exactly right in every accusation that you bring against me, but you are accusing the brothers and sisters who conquer you 'by the blood of the Lamb and the word of their testimony'" (see Rev. 12:11). As guilty but forgiven sinners, what the powers and principalities of this age say to us is true. But we've already been accused; we've already been indicted; we've been arrested; we've been dressed in purple and beaten; we've been stapled to a Roman cross; we've had the wrath of God poured out upon us; we've been left in a tomb as a bloated, abandoned, cursed corpse; and on a Sunday morning in Jerusalem, we were resurrected.

So when the accusations of the Evil One come against us, what he hears in reply is the gospel truth that we can't be re-executed. What we hear said of us from the Father is, "This is my beloved Son in whom I am well pleased," because we are in union with Christ, and what is true of him is now, by the grace of God, true of us. And that is precisely why "there is therefore now *no condemnation* for those who are in Christ Jesus" (Rom. 8:1).

Heaven's Satellite Campus

When we gather as a church, then, we don't come together as former sinners. We don't come together as regular people. We come as the crucified. And when we join in worship, we are joining with an already existing worship in the heavenly places. We're just an earthly satellite campus.

Many of us like to go to conferences because it's encouraging to be around a group of like-minded people. It's encouraging to hear thousands of believers singing together in worship, when what you typically hear each week are just those few voices in your rural church, in that abandoned part of town where it's hard to attract visitors. But what we need to remember is that, every single Lord's Day when we gather together, we are joining—by the eyes and ears of faith—a number no man can count. We are joining with a global, trans-generational movement, and we stand with the redeemed of all the ages with the confession that we are lost but he was slain, and with his blood he has purchased a church. And this church is a church that corrects, a church that rebukes, a church that transforms—because it speaks not with the voice of self-sufficiency but with the royal, transforming voice of the Lord Jesus Christ.

Jesus Will Build His Church

Jesus is going to build his church, and the gates of hell cannot stop it. Yet we often wonder whether our churches are functioning well enough to produce the next Charles Spurgeon or the next Billy Graham. But the truth of the matter is, the next Billy Graham might be drunk right now. The next Spurgeon might be selling drugs on a street corner right at this moment. Jesus never promised that he would raise up a people from our established ranks.

What he promised is that he would bring out of the world and all of sinful humanity a church, a people in every single generation. He will build it with ex-fisherman and ex–tax collectors. He will build it with ex-terrorists, and ex-fornicators, and ex-adulterers, and ex-murderers. And we will testify that though our power is not enough, Jesus is Lord, and he will build his church.

Over a Reptile's Skull

When we gather together, we announce in all our little places that the kingdom of God has drawn near to us in Christ. When we gather around the Lord's Table, we participate in a foretaste of a future banquet at the marriage supper of the Lamb. When we watch that new believer being baptized, we are seeing the kingdom of God uprooting the kingdom of darkness. And when we receive the word of proclamation given in our assembly—whether in sermon, song, spoken encouragement, or gentle rebuke—we participate in the answering of the promise that Jesus would build his church over a reptile's skull.

As we grow in Christ, we see that the kingdom of God will come in fullness—and this kingdom is not just a manner of eating and drinking, not just a matter of evangelizing and congregating. The kingdom of God does not consist in talk but in power. So in the church, when we see something, we say something—with the commission of Christ our king.

Conclusion

Act the Miracle

*Future Grace, the Word of the Cross, and
the Purifying Power of God's Promises*

John Piper

When God predestined his people to be *conformed to the image of his Son* (Rom. 8:29), and when "he chose us in him before the foundation of the world, that we should be *holy*" (Eph. 1:4), what is clear is that he intended that someday the world would be filled with the beauty of his holiness—or, to say it another way, the glory of God. Someday it will be a world of people, created and recreated in his image, in the likeness of his Son. It will be a world filled with the glory of the Lord the way the waters cover the sea. It will be a world radiant with the beauty of holiness.

The Breathtaking Beauty of Holiness

I know that, for some of us, the biblical vision of holiness is too new and too strange to fully realize what is meant by the beauty of holiness—the beauty of sanctification. So let me give you one person's effort to put into words the beauty of holiness. To my knowledge, no one has done this better than Jonathan Edwards:

> We drink in strange notions of holiness from our childhood, as if it were a melancholy, morose, sour, and unpleasant thing; but there is nothing in it but what is sweet and ravishingly lovely. 'Tis the highest

beauty and amiableness, vastly above all other beauties. 'Tis a divine beauty, makes the soul heavenly and far purer than anything here on earth. . . . 'Tis of a sweet, pleasant, charming, lovely, amiable, delightful, serene, calm, and still nature. 'Tis almost too high a beauty for any creatures to be adorned with; it makes the soul a little, sweet, and delightful image of the blessed Jehovah.

Oh, how may angels stand, with pleased, delighted, and charmed eyes, and look and look, with smiles of pleasure upon their lips, upon that soul that is holy; how may they hover over such a soul, to delight to behold such loveliness! . . . What a sweet calmness, what a calm ecstasy, doth it bring to the soul! How doth it make the soul love itself; how doth it make the pure invisible world love it; yea, how doth God love it and delight in it; how do even the whole creation, the sun, the fields, and trees love a humble holiness; how doth all the world congratulate, embrace, and sing to a sanctified soul! . . .

It makes the soul like a delightful field or garden planted by God . . . where the sun is Jesus Christ; the blessed beams and calm breeze, the Holy Spirit; the sweet and delightful flowers, and the pleasant shrill music of the little birds, are the Christian graces.

Or like the little white flower: pure, unspotted, and undefiled, low and humble, pleasing and harmless; receiving the beams, the pleasant beams of the serene sun, gently moved and a little shaken by a sweet breeze, rejoicing as it were in a calm rapture, diffusing around [a] most delightful fragrancy, standing most peacefully and lovingly in the midst of the other like flowers round about.[1]

What is this beauty of holiness in God? It is the infinite worth of his transcendent Trinitarian fullness, along with the perfect harmony between that worth and all his feeling and thinking and acting. None of God's acts contradicts the supreme value of his transcendent fullness. There is perfect consistency. Without exception and without interruption, God's acts perfectly express the value of his fullness. The beauty of God's holiness is this perfect harmony between all that God does and the infinite value of all that God is.

[1] Jonathan Edwards, *The "Miscellanies" (Entry Nos. a-z, aa-zz, 1–500)*, in *The Works of Jonathan Edwards*, vol. 13, ed. Harry Stout (New Haven, CT: Yale University Press, 1994), 163–64.

The Beauty of Holiness *in Us*

The beauty of holiness in us is similar. "Be holy, for I am holy" (1 Pet. 1:16), God says to us. God is disciplining us, Hebrews says, "that we may share his holiness" (Heb. 12:10)—this divine holiness. Which means that the beauty of holiness in God's children is the harmony between our lives and the infinite value of all God is. When our lives gladly express the value of God's all-satisfying fullness, we are holy. And we are beautiful. The only thing ugly—the only thing bad—in the world is the failure to reflect the infinite value of all that God is. But wherever our emotions and thoughts and deeds show forth the all-satisfying fullness of God, there is the beauty of holiness.

Some day this is what will fill the whole earth. Someday all that is unholy will be cast into outer darkness. The saints of God—the holy ones—will shine like the sun in the kingdom of their father (Matt. 13:43). They will obtain what Paul calls "the freedom of the glory of the children of God" (Rom. 8:21)—freedom from all unholiness and all misery. Then the whole creation, Paul says, will be made to conform to the beauty of the holiness of the children of God. In that new universe of God's recreation, there will be perfect harmony—perfect concord—between the natural world, and the fullness of human life, and the infinite worth of the fullness of God. Everything, every emotion, every thought, every act will perfectly testify to the infinite worth of God's transcendent fullness. The redeemed universe will be filled with the beauty of holiness.

A Divine Miracle in Us

Until that day, we are in the grand process called sanctification, or glorification, or becoming holy as God is holy. What I want to show in this final chapter is that this process is a divine miracle in you, and you act the miracle. God is wholly engaged in bringing your life and this world to its appointed destiny of holiness. And this full engagement of God in the process of your sanctification is no limitation on *your* engagement, but is, in fact, the creation of your engagement. He *works* the miracle of sanctification; you *act* the miracle. He produces it; you perform it. If you don't use your will to act the miracle, there is no miracle. God's sovereign enablement of holiness does not contradict the act of duty; it creates it.

- When God opens the eyes of the blind, it is the blind who see.
- When God gives strength to shriveled legs, it is the lame who do the walking.
- When God touches the ears of the deaf, it is the deaf who do the hearing.
- When God calls Lazarus from the grave, it is Lazarus who walks out on his own two feet.
- When God changes Zacchaeus's heart, it is Zacchaeus who gives back fourfold what he had stolen.
- When God fills you with compassion, it is you who exercises your will to feed the hungry and clothe the naked and visit the prison and take in the refugee.
- When God gives you merciful humility, it is you who turns the other cheek.
- When God inclines your heart to his Word, it is you who gets out of bed early in the morning to read your Bible.
- When God gives you courage and love, it is you who shares Christ with your neighbor.
- When God puts a generous spirit in you, you are the one who writes the extra check for the ministry of the church.
- When God gives you a patient confidence in his timing, you are the one who drives the speed limit and stops at stop signs and buckles your seatbelt.
- When God makes you content with his provision, it's you who tells the truth on your tax returns.
- When God makes his glory more satisfying than lust, it's you who turns away from pornography.
- When God gives you a sweet satisfaction in your future reward, you are the one who blesses your enemies and does not curse them.

God authors the miracle of sanctification, and you act the miracle.

God Authors All, We Act All

Here's the way Jonathan Edwards describes God's sanctifying grace and power in our lives:

> We are not merely passive in it, nor yet does God do some and we do the rest, but God does all and we do all. God produces all and we act all. For that is what he produces, our own acts. God is the only proper author and fountain; we only are the proper actors. We are in different respects wholly passive and wholly active.[2]

This is what I want to try to shed light on from the Bible in this chapter: God producing our holiness, and we acting our holiness; God as the author of the miracle of sanctification, we as the actors of the miracle of our sanctification. How does the Bible teach this? And how do we experience it in real life?

It Is Crucial We Start with the Cross

Let's start with the cross of Christ. God cancels our sins at the cross through faith alone, so that we can then conquer our sins by the Holy Spirit. Or, to use doctrinal language, the enjoyment of justification must precede the energy of sanctification. It is crucial that we start with the cross. If we reverse the order of justification by faith alone and sanctification by the Spirit, we have another religion, not Christianity.

When Charles Wesley taught us to sing, "He breaks the power of canceled sin" (from the hymn "O for a Thousand Tongues to Sing"), he was teaching the fundamental truth about how the cross relates to sanctification. The cross cancels sins for all who believe on Jesus. Then on the basis of that cancellation of our sins, God breaks the power of our actual sinning. It's not the other way around. There would be no gospel, and no music, if we tried to sing, "He cancels the guilt of conquered sins." No, first the cancellation. Then the conquering.

---

[2] Jonathan Edwards, *Writings on the Trinity, Grace, and Faith*, in *The Works of Jonathan Edwards*, vol. 21, ed. Sang Hyun Lee (New Haven, CT: Yale University Press, 2003), 251.

Defeating Pardoned Sins

Here is one New Testament example of how this works. Paul says in Romans 6:5, "We have been united with [Christ] in a death like his." That's how our sins were canceled. When Christ died, we died (2 Cor. 5:14). He suffered the condemnation for our sins (Rom. 8:3), and by union with him through faith, our sins are canceled. They are already punished, condemned.

On that basis, Paul commands us in Romans 6:12 to act: "Let not sin therefore reign in your mortal body." *Your sin is canceled because of union with Christ. Now, dethrone it. Break the power of canceled sin.* So the death of Christ in our place is always foundational for our defeat of sin. The basis for our conquering sin is always Christ's canceling sin. Or to say it another way, the only sin that we can defeat in practice is a pardoned sin. Or to say it another way, the pursuit of sanctification can only happen on the foundation of justification.

If we try to defeat an uncanceled sin, a sin that is not already covered by the blood of Jesus—that is, if we try to conquer our sin before it is canceled—we become our own saviors; we nullify the justification of the ungodly (Rom. 4:4–5); and we head straight for despair and suicide.

Canceling Sin Precedes Conquering Sin

Here are two other examples from the New Testament. (1) "You were bought with a price. So glorify God in your body" (1 Cor. 6:20). (2) "[Forgive] one another, as God in Christ forgave you" (Eph. 4:32). Canceling sin precedes conquering sin. When the cross cancels the condemning power of our unholiness, it doesn't make battle for holiness superfluous; it makes it possible. And in the end, it makes it totally successful.

So now we find ourselves loved by God, accepted, adopted into his family, forgiven for all our sins, and justified—all because of Christ. In this condition of profound security and assurance, the Bible says to us, Pursue "the holiness without which no one will see the Lord" (Heb. 12:14). "Strive to enter through the narrow door. For many, I tell you, will seek to enter and will not be able" (Luke 13:24). "Whoever says 'I know him' but does not keep his commandments is a liar, and the truth is not in him" (1 John 2:4). In other words, conquering canceled sin is essential if we are to be finally saved. Not because sins can be uncanceled, but because the will to kill canceled sin is the necessary sign that it is canceled.

How Do We Act the Miracle?

The questions before us now are, *How* do we go about "pursuing the holiness without which no one will see the Lord"? How do we "strive to enter through the narrow door"? How do we "keep the commandments"? How do we dethrone and kill canceled sin?

Let's consider a sequence of passages that answer these questions. First, Romans 8:13 (which is the basis of John Owen's book *The Mortification of Sin*): "If you live according to the flesh you will die, but if by the Spirit you put to death the deeds of the body, you will live." Here, imbedded in the greatest chapter on assurance in all the Bible, the Great Eight of Romans, is in verse 13 a warning that if we surrender to the flesh and decide we don't want to make war on sin anymore, we will perish. We will show that our sins were never canceled.

"By the Spirit"

What is the alternative to that surrender and that death? "But if by the Spirit you put to death the deeds of the body, you will live." So our first answer to the questions, *How do you pursue holiness? How do you strive for the narrow door? How do you dethrone and kill sin?* is, you do it "by the Spirit." "If *by the Spirit* you put to death the deeds of the body, you will live."

Continuous, Sustained, Strenuous Effort

Now put alongside that Philippians 2:12–13: "Therefore, my beloved, as you have always obeyed, so now, not only as in my presence but much more in my absence, work out your own salvation with fear and trembling, *for it is God who works in you, both to will and to work for his good pleasure.*"

When Paul says "work out your own salvation," the word (Greek *katergazesthe*) means "produce it," "bring it about," "effect it."[3] Commentator Peter O'Brien sums it up with the words, "continuous, sustained, strenuous effort." As dangerous as this language is, it is biblical. "Bring about your salvation." "Produce your salvation." "Effect your salvation by continuous, sustained, strenuous, effort."

Act Your Salvation from Sin

Don't let salvation remain a vague, distant outcome. Let it be the daily deliverances from sin. This is our salvation—salvation from sin. So daily produce salvation from sinning. Act your deliverance. Act your victory. Act your dethroning and killing of sin.

Act your deliverance from anger, resentment, fear of man, discouragement, self-pity, self-promotion, hardness, envy, moodiness, sulking, indifference to suffering, laziness, boredom, passiveness, lack of praising others, lack of joy in Jesus, and more. All these need daily killing.

How? Just as Romans 8:13 says, "by the Spirit" put sin to death. So Philippians 2:12–13 says bring about your own salvation from sinning, "for it is God who works in you, both to will and to work for his good pleasure." Pick up your sin-killing sword, because God is picking it up with your hands. Wield it because God is wielding it with your hands. Thrust sin through with it, because God is thrusting him through with it. Act the miracle of sin-killing sanctification, for God is willing and doing it in you. This is the mystery of sanctification. "I worked harder than any of them, though it was not I, but the grace of God that is with me" (1 Cor. 15:10). The work of Paul was a wonder of grace. Oh, did he work! And when he was done, he said it was all of God—all of grace.

---

[3] Romans 5:3: "Suffering *produces* endurance." Romans 7:8: "Sin *produced* in me covetousness." 2 Corinthians 4:17: "Affliction is *producing* a weight of glory." 2 Corinthians 7:10: "Worldly grief *produces* death." James 1:3: "The testing of your faith *produces* steadfastness."

How Do We Tap into the Power?

Which leads now to the question, *How do we consciously tap into God's miracle-working power in our lives?* If it is "by the Spirit" that we kill sin and pursue holiness, and if it is by God's willing and working in us that we will and work for holiness, how do we connect with the divine Spirit who wills our willing and works our working?

Paul answers us in Galatians 3:5: "Does he who supplies the Spirit to you and works miracles among you do so by works of the law, or by hearing with faith?" The answer is that the miracle-working Spirit is supplied to us, and active in us, by *hearing with faith.* God wills and works in us to defeat sin and produce holiness through the hearing of faith. We hear God speak, and we believe him, and in and through that believing, the sin-killing, holiness-creating power of God produces the miracle that we act.

Blood-Bought Promises for Our Situation

Let's get even more specific. As I read the New Testament, the pervasive focus of that sanctifying faith[4] is faith in future grace, that is, faith in all that God promises to be for us in Jesus because of what he did for us on the cross. In other words, the way we tap into the power of God for the miracle of sin-killing sanctification is by hearing a blood-bought promise of God for our situation, and by believing it, that is, by receiving it and embracing it as a treasure more precious than the pleasures of the temptation in front of us.

In other words, as the Holy Spirit awakens and moves through that faith in God's promise, the power of canceled sin is broken. It is dethroned. It loses its compelling force because, by the Spirit, faith embraces God's promise as more satisfying. The power of canceled sin is broken by the power of a superior pleasure. And faith is the soul's embrace of that superior pleasure.

---

[4] See Acts 26:18: "I am sending you to open their eyes, so that they may turn from darkness to light and from the power of Satan to God, that they may receive forgiveness of sins and a place among those who are *sanctified by faith in me.*" See also 2 Corinthians 5:7 and Galatians 2:20 where the new life of the believer is lived "through faith" or "by faith."

Made Plain in Hebrews

No book of the Bible makes this more plain than the book of Hebrews. What is faith, according to the book of Hebrews? "Now faith is the assurance of things hoped for, the conviction of things not seen" (Heb. 11:1). The assurance of things hoped for. Faith is future-oriented. And the future it hopes for is the promise of Hebrews 11:6: "Without faith it is impossible to please him, for whoever would draw near to God must believe that he exists and that he rewards those who seek him." So faith that pleases God believes God is and that he is preparing us for great, all-compensating, all-satisfying reward.

That expectation of an all-satisfying reward is why faith taps into the power of the Spirit to produce the beauty of holiness. Watch how it works in the case of Moses in Hebrews 11:24–26:

> *By faith* Moses, when he was grown up, refused to be called the son of Pharaoh's daughter, choosing rather to be mistreated with the people of God than to enjoy the fleeting pleasures of sin. He considered the reproach of Christ greater wealth than the treasures of Egypt, for he was looking to the reward.

How does the Holy Spirit kill sin and produce the beauty of holiness in Moses? He does it "by faith." "*By faith* Moses refused to be called the son of Pharaoh's daughter." And what was that faith? It was the assurance of things hoped for. Verse 26: "He was looking to the reward." So faith embraces the reward of all God promises to be for us, and in comparison with that, the wealth of Egypt looks puny and the pleasures of Egypt look fleeting, and Moses receives the power to see the mission of leading this people as thrilling, and he acts the miracle of the beauty of holiness.

Having a Better Possession

Centuries later the same thing happened to the early Christians mentioned in Hebrews 10:34. How did they kill the sin of fear and greed and selfishness? How did they act the miracle of the beauty of compassion and risk their lives to visit their friends in prison? They did it by faith in future grace. That is, they did it by the assurance of things hoped for. "You had compassion on those in prison, and you joyfully accepted the plundering of your property, since you knew that you yourselves had a better possession and an abiding one."

How did they tap into such beautiful holiness-producing power? "Does he who supplies the Spirit to you and works miracles among you do so by works of the law, or by hearing with faith?" (Gal. 3:5). They heard a promise such as Psalm 16:11: "In [God's] presence there is fullness of joy; at [his] right hand are pleasures forevermore." They embraced this promise of all that God would be for them in Jesus, and the certainty and greatness and extent of this promised reward broke the power of canceled fear and canceled greed and canceled selfishness. They were given the power to act the miracle of the beauty of holiness, the beauty of mercy and compassion, as they risked their possessions and their lives for the all-satisfying reward of God.

On and on the Scriptures go, giving promise after promise of God's future grace, and breaking the power of sin after sin, and compelling believers into more and more beautiful holiness.

Harmony between Our Lives and God's Value

Which brings us back to where we started. I argued at the beginning of this chapter that the beauty of holiness in God's children is the harmony, or the concord, between our lives and the infinite value of all God is. And I said that God predestined us to holiness because his aim is that earth be filled with the beauty of holiness—the expression of the infinite worth of his transcendent fullness.

On the way to that predestined beauty, we have seen that God canceled the sins of his people by the death of his Son. Then he commanded that we break the power of this canceled sin—that we kill sin and pursue holiness. Then he instructed us to act the miracle of holiness by the power of the Spirit, and to do so because he is at work in us to will and to do this very miracle. He authors it; we act it. Then he showed us that we tap into this sanctifying, sin-killing, holiness-producing power by the hearing of faith—by hearing all that God promises to be for us in Jesus, and embracing this as our supremely satisfying treasure.

The Beauty of Holiness Filling the Earth

Now we can see how this grand process of sanctification is leading us to the predestined glory where the beauty of holiness fills the earth. God has ordained that all the obedience of sanctification—all our holiness—be the obedience of faith, because faith is the soul's embrace of the infinite worth of the transcendent fullness of the triune God. Which means that at the heart of all Christian obedience, there is an act of the human soul in harmony with the supreme worth of God. This is what makes all Christian obedience holy obedience, which is why one day the earth will be filled with the beauty of holiness. It will be filled with saints.

There will be in the soul of every saint, and in all their outward action, a perfect harmony with the infinite worth of God's transcendent fullness. Within there will be the soul's full satisfaction with all that God is for us in Jesus, and without will be the fruit of that faith in perfect love. In that way, the earth will be filled with the beauty of holiness.

Appendix

Conversation with the Contributors

Kevin DeYoung, Russell Moore, John Piper, Ed Welch, Jarvis Williams, and David Mathis

The following is a lightly edited transcript of the panel discussion held on September 29, 2012, at the Desiring God National Conference, where the chapters of this book were originally delivered. David Mathis's questions are in italics.

Jarvis, thank you for taking us in a practical direction with your message. Would you, and the others on the panel, have anything more to add here in terms of some practicalities of when you go about pursuing personal devotional and prayer time, how you go about that?

Jarvis Williams: I'm an early-to-bed, early-to-rise type of person. I love to wake up at five or six o'clock in the morning and have long seasons of prayer, Scripture reading, and meditation. In addition to that, I try to incorporate prayer and reflection and preaching to myself throughout the course of the day. But I like to have an early morning season of prayer before I start my day.

There's flexibility in terms of individual persons and temperaments. Some people stay up later and sleep later and find their best time in prayer and Bible reading to be in the evening. Others find it perhaps in the afternoon, depending on their schedule.

John Piper: The principle that we should keep in mind is that the warfare against sin, and for holiness, is a warfare to be fought in the moment with the Bible and in the background with the Bible. In other words, daily meditation on Scripture is tilling the garden in which the flowers of holiness grow. And if a rabbit comes along at three o'clock in the afternoon and tries to chew down this beautiful flower, you kill it, and you kill it with a verse that you remembered from the morning. So it's both/and. Sometimes we fall into the trap of doing only one. We say we need the Bible at the moment when we're challenged in some way of impatience or unkindness, and I need a verse to kill that sin, yes, you do. I do. And I also need to be stocking that arsenal and sweetening my sour heart every morning.

So note those two things by way of principle. We are pursuing a sweetening, humbling, nourishing, strengthening—those are just adjectives of which there are probably a thousand in God's mind of things he's doing in our heart when we read the Bible that we don't know he's doing. And then through the day we need particular daggers that we stick Satan with when he's trying to make us do something we shouldn't do.

Jarvis Williams: That reminds me of something practical that I've experienced in terms of having a consistent time of prayer. There was a season in my life when I had doubts about whether God's sovereignty was worth believing. I would be seized with anxiety unexpectedly, and start fighting, preaching to myself key verses. I had to fight, and that fight was late at night, throughout the wee hours of the morning. The seasons of life we're in sometimes push us to fight in a less conventional way in terms of when we have our devotions. Maybe it's the early hours of the morning, or late at night, or midday. When we struggle, we fight in the struggle at the moment.

Kevin DeYoung: I'll add two things quickly. First, don't pass up God's promptings to pray. As an order guy, a Presbyterian type, sometimes I'll get this feeling, *I just need to go pray*, and then the thought comes to mind, *I do that in the morning*. No, just do that now.

The second thing—very practically—that has helped my prayer life is not sitting down while I'm praying. I walk most of the time, whether it's on a treadmill, which I find extremely tedious, or outside in Michigan, which I find very cold. But I just walk. It's much harder to fall asleep walking than sitting, studies have shown. I wish that I could wake up and sit there and just have great times of prayer, but I get very great times of sleepiness that come quickly. So I walk, and you go out and you walk 25 minutes, and you have 25 minutes to come back, or however long it is, and you pray, and your mind wanders at times and then you come back and in some of the wandering you get some great things that come in and out of there. Walking has helped me immensely.

Russell Moore: Walking has helped me as well. Also it helps me personally to keep from becoming stilted and scripted in prayer, because as you're walking, your mind tends to move around and race. It becomes easier for me not to move into some kind of theatrical mode of prayer. The most important thing is to know yourself and to know how to subvert yourself and your particular weaknesses and tendencies toward sin.

When it comes to the memorization of Scripture, for instance, I have a friend who can memorize entire books of the Bible. He does it on note cards, and you can reference Ephesians 4:3 and almost see the notecards turning in his mind. He's built with an engineer's mind where it seems easier for him to do. I have to trick myself into memorizing Scripture. I have more of a literary kind of a mind, and so I'll have a lot of Scripture memorized, but it's not because I've done note cards. It's just because I've spent so much time in that particular place. So I don't think you can look at any particular model and say you're necessarily going to emulate that, as much as you have to say, "Where am I weak? Where am I strong?" and then build around that in those practices.

Ed Welch: I think I'm one of the few completely undisciplined Presbyterians. I know that walking around is helpful for prayer, but so what? It doesn't matter. I'd still rather just sit in my chair.

How does Scripture affect my sanctification? It's like working out. I never notice it day to day, but it does something over time. I know that. I've tried getting up, and it just never works. I just try to do it.

There are a few things we haven't mentioned yet. You didn't include when your wife really yells at you about something. I think that's a moment we need spiritual discipline. In my own style of life, if you followed me around, I guess like most of us, I don't do obvious sins. I'm not screaming at people. I'm not involved in pornography. It's easy for me to go through a day without being pierced by the Spirit that I didn't have times of confession. So I know that my wife's confrontations—whether sweet or not—are oftentimes exactly what I need. And those are times the Spirit uses in my life very powerfully, along with what you mentioned—just the hardships of life, the failures of life, the tragedies we see around us.

One more thing to add here: I do find that for me, Scripture and prayer corporately are most helpful. To do it with other people—with my spouse, with my kids, with my colleagues—that's when I find the Spirit meets us with any kind of discipline.

Would there be any additional means of grace than what we've mentioned so far that you'd like to commend to others?

Kevin DeYoung: The Lord's Supper. Our church's liturgy says that the Lord's Supper is a feast of remembrance, communion, and hope. God condescends to us by giving us visual aids. People say we live in a visual culture. You need to see something. You need to taste it and touch it. Well, that's true, and God thought of that, and so he gave us "sacraments" or "ordinances" for something to see as a tangible reminder. As the Heidelberg Catechism says, "As surely as I can taste this bread and drink from this cup, so surely did Christ die on the cross." When you come bearing the weight of your sin on Sunday morning, you may wonder, *Can God love me? Can God forgive me?* You should respond, *Can I eat this bread? Can I drink from this cup?* So there's a precious means of grace for us at the Table that we often overlook.

John Piper: There is also the inspiration of other people's holiness. I'm thinking right now of history and biographies. They can be a means of grace. For me, few things outside the Bible inspire me to want to be something that I'm not as biographies of people who, in all their sinfulness, have conquered some sin or conquered some weakness and have glorified Christ more because of it. So I'm stirred to want to press on and fight the daily fight of faith by stories that I read in history of people who have done it.

Russell Moore: And hymnody. I find that often the power of hymns and songs comes not in the moment in which I'm singing them but later when they just sort of show up some primal place inside of me— often very, very convicting. I found myself just a few weeks ago, as I was driving along, having a very difficult time in terms of self-pity and anxiety about something, and I had my iPod set to random music. All of a sudden an old hymn from my tradition came on, "Just As I Am," which I'd heard every single Sunday—so many verses of it—at the end of every service as a child. But it just pierced through to me because I thought, *I don't believe that right now I'm standing here just as I am without one plea except that your blood was shed for me.* And I was moved to the point of repentance and conviction that I'm not sure simply thinking about it would have gotten to me so quickly. And so I think hymnody is significant and important with lasting hymns that reach to that deep place inside of you. I think that's critically important.

John gave us a few categories of spiritual disciplines—feeding ourselves in the moment of temptation. Over lunch today we were talking about

James 1. Let me read those verses and rehash some of that conversation on temptation.

> *Let no one say when he is tempted, "I am being temped by God," for God cannot be tempted with evil, and he himself tempts no one. But each person is tempted when he is lured and enticed by his own desire. Then desire when it has conceived gives birth to sin, and sin when it is fully grown brings forth death. (vv. 13–15)*

What kind of counsel do you give to Christians for the moment of temptation?

Russell Moore: Scripture shows that Satan works in two ways. One of them is deception. He deceives people into thinking their sinning won't have consequences. "You will not surely die." Or he leads them to think, "I'm special. God's law doesn't apply to me in this case." So they're deceived, and they don't see what's actually happening until it's too late. The other way he works is through accusation. The Devil accuses us because of our sin. Both of those areas—deception and accusation—lead to the same place, which is ultimately death.

One problem we have in the moment of temptation is not being aware of the darkness around us. Scripture warns us consistently. The passage that Jarvis mentioned earlier about the cosmic powers of this present darkness—be aware of that. Be aware of your own fallenness. Be aware of your own tendency toward sin. But also be aware of the possibility of despair. One of the ways that Satan can pin us down in temptation is to have us start to think of ourselves as an animal. *I don't have any power over this. I don't have any control over this. I'm just simply determined to walk in this way.*

What we were talking about at lunch today is that I had a guy come to see me one time. I'll never forget the conversation. He said, "There's no way I can be a Christian because I'm just grappling with things all the time. I'm struggling all the time." And I said, "Me, too." He said, "Oh, no, you don't understand. I'm always at war inside of myself."

I said, "Me, too." He said again, "No, you don't understand. Let me tell you. This is what I mean. If you could prove to me today that the bones of Jesus are in the ground in the Middle East, I would leave here and get as drunk as I could get, have every drug I could find, and sleep with any woman that would let me." I said, "Me, too. As a matter of fact, the Bible says that's exactly what we ought to do if Christ has not been raised! But do you believe that the bones of Jesus are in the ground in the Middle East?" And he said, "No. That's the reason why I'm constantly in this turmoil and fighting against this inside myself." And I had to say, "What you're living is the normal Christian life."

What he assumed was that everybody else is living this life of tranquility and humming hymns to themselves internally. And he knew the kind of struggle that he had. Well, that's evidence of the Spirit's work. He wasn't able to see *the difference between temptation and sin.* And God does promise you through the gospel and through the Spirit the power to escape from sin. God never promises us an escape from all temptation until our resurrection from the dead. And so if we don't see temptation as something we're going to have to take up our cross and fight against, then we're not going to be armed and able to stand.

John Piper: Do you ever sing the hymn "Blessed Assurance"? The second verse says, "Perfect submission, all is at rest. I in my Savior am happy and blessed." I mean, this is a serious question. I stumble over the hymn wondering, *Can I think of an instance where that's true so I could with some integrity sing this song?* Because I like the tune, and I like most of the words. But perfect submission? All is at rest? I in my Savior am happy and blessed? My answer is that there are moments like that, I think. So do you agree with that?

Russell Moore: I think those moments are small and fleeting, and yet the whole of the Christian life is one of battle because there's always the presence of sin, and there's always the presence of the world, the flesh, and the Devil around me that I'm to put to death inside of myself.

And so I think that if somebody is expecting a life of tranquility rather than a life of peace—in Scripture, peace in this age doesn't necessarily mean tranquility ("the God of peace will crush Satan beneath your feet")—if you're expecting that kind of lack of self-crucifixion, you're expecting something Jesus doesn't promise. And I think so many of us do, and we want that to be the case. This may largely be due to some of the ways that we have given testimonies in our churches, in our conferences, and in our evangelistic crusades. We want to encourage people, so we want to say to that drug addict out there, *There's hope for you.* So what do we do? We put up an ex-drug addict who says, "Previously I loved heroin. Then I met Jesus. Now I'm totally free from that. I haven't thought about heroin in years." And we think that's going to be an encouragement.

The problem is you have that guy who's sitting out there who says, "I've been following Christ for fifteen years, and every morning I get up and have to fight against this pull toward heroin." He thinks that's a sign of lack of godliness, when in reality that's a sign of godliness. The ones who are tranquil and simply marching forward with no thought of anything going on internally—I think Hebrews 12 would tell us they are those who are being left alone. The Devil is not disturbing them. They're on their way to destruction and not being disciplined by the Spirit.

As long as you see that second verse of "Blessed Assurance" in an eschatological sense—I have this rest, I have this peace, I have this tranquility in Christ seated at the right hand of the Father—but don't translate it into our own kind of prosperity gospel where God's favor with you is seen as an absence of any kind of conflict, then I think we can sing it with integrity.

Ed Welch: Since you guys say so much packed into a little bit, let me try to make some of the links, because I think they're important. We're talking about temptation. The first thing Russ talked about was Satan, which was brilliant. That's the way we're to be thinking. And then you come up with this song which says, as far as I understand what you were saying, we know his devices. And what's the way to do battle with Satan? It's to humble ourselves before the Lord. Perhaps if there's one short statement summary of how to do battle, it's this: *God, you are God*, or *God, you are holy*. To submit ourselves to the Lord encapsulates so much of the battle. John and Russ, the two of you are saying all kinds of things that are very important. And then you're coming back and reminding us that we're perfectionists at heart. That's our theology. It's on-off. We once sinned, and now we're perfect. And this whole conference is moving us toward what's called "progressive sanctification." Sin doesn't let go of its clutches immediately. And that wonderful phrase we move from an *affection for sin* to *sin being an affliction*—and that's a process. So, thanks. You guys are saying lots of helpful things in just those short comments.

Kevin DeYoung: Let me just give the J. C. Ryle line, that the Christian has two great marks about him—his inner peace and his inner warfare. And both of those things are true. When we read from 1 John, "His commands are not burdensome," do we not think, *Really?* But they're not. And the yoke is easy, and the burden is light, and the warfare is long and unceasing. And that's the whole Christian life: how all of those things fit together.

I love what Russ is saying about temptation, because I think a lot of Christians are rather unaware of temptation, so they fall into sin. If you're not aware of temptation in your life, it's not because you're not being tempted. You're just sinning. You're just giving in to it. But, on the other hand, I think Christians could have a lot of false guilt and think, *I'm unclean because, man, there's this part of me or there's Satan coming at me and making me feel like I want to do these things that I know are not good.* And as I said, assuming that King David was not going onto the roof because he knew what was coming, he went onto the roof, sees Bathsheba, something clicks, and there's temptation. There's some moment. Maybe it's just a split second there for David that's not sin but is very pregnant with sin, and it becomes sin very quickly. We need to realize there are those moments of temptation all the time in our lives and address them and flee from them. Being tempted doesn't mean we have sinned, but if we don't fight, if we don't resist, we will sin.

John should chime in here about the 1 Corinthians 10 escape from temptation.

John Piper: I'll just draw attention to the word *endure*: "No temptation has befallen you but what is common to man, and with it the Lord will make a way of escape that you may *endure* it." I've always thought it's a really provocative way to end—with the word *endure*—just after he's used the word *escape*. A way of escape is made that you may *endure*? Wouldn't it seem that if you found an escape, then you wouldn't need to be enduring anymore? But my conclusion is that *the escape is the power to endure.* So the temptation keeps coming. A temptation is being pressed upon you, but you're not being crushed. I'm feeling pressed by an external or internal something, and endurance means I'm not giving in. I'm not going to squash. And that's the escape. The Lord gives that.

Ed Welch: One other comment on God's commandments not being burdensome. Perhaps one of the things we could add to our struggle with temptation is something like this: one of the most human things we can do is experience temptation that is palpable and say no in such a way that it's painful to say no. So we can add to the escape and the endurance, "And we're going to love it," because that's who we were created to be. We're going to love that particular battle. We can. That's the way we can invite people to the battle. It's not burdensome. It's a delight because you will know what it means to be fully human, and you'll love it.

What is the role, or not the role, of commandments in sanctification? Would anyone want to address "the third use of the law"?

Kevin DeYoung: Theologians talk about the law being used in different ways. One way is as a restraint on wickedness. God gives us his commandments, and there is with them a kind of common grace that restrains us from doing everything we might want to do. Second, what we think of most in distinguishing between law and gospel is that the commands show us what we don't live up to. I don't love my neighbor as myself. I don't love God with all my heart, soul, mind, and strength. I don't obey the Ten Commandments. I need a Savior. The law shows you your need for a Savior. You run to Christ.

The "third use," which we find in the various historically Reformed confessions—and also in the Lutheran ones, which is sometimes overlooked—is that the law is also given to us as the perfect rule of righteousness (how we should live). There are many difficult theological layers, like, what do we mean by the law? For example, the law could mean the Torah, the first five books of the Bible. It can mean the Mosaic covenant. It can mean just commands. And what do we mean as an "instrument" of our sanctification?

The law does not give us the power to obey, but it does give us the blueprint. It is pointing us along the path. It is telling us how we ought to live, so that in 1 Corinthians 9 Paul can do this back-and-forth about not being "under the law" but being "under the law of Christ." He's saying the Mosaic covenant is not our covenant. We're not "under law," and yet the new covenant doesn't do away with commandments. We're still under "the law of Christ." So when Paul gets to Romans 13, for example, he talks about love. He says, "Love is fulfilled in these commandments." And for "these commandments," he lists half of the Decalogue as fulfilled in love.

So if people want to know what it looks like to love your neighbor, you have to go to some of the commandments. And if you really want to obey the commandments, you have to talk about loving your neighbor. You shouldn't quite say they're interchangeable, but you have to talk about both if you're going to talk about either in a truly biblical way. That is the heart of the third use of the law.

As for commands—the New Testament's full of them. God still gives commands in the new covenant. We just need to obey them as one hoping to live out all that we are in Christ and not as one hoping to prove ourselves or hoping to earn some sort of status before God. So the law leads to gospel. But if you look at the exodus, the gospel also leads to law, because he set them free from Egypt. God didn't tell them clean up your act. He didn't say, "Obey the Ten Commandments for four hundred years, and then I'll set you free." He just set them free, and then he led them to Sinai and said, "Now you're going to worship me, and here's what it looks like."

What is the role of striving in the Christian life, and how are we to think about the Christian "striving" when we come across biblical texts that command it?

Russell Moore: Kevin got at this very well in his message this morning [chapter 2]. There is a tendency, and there is a danger, because we as Christians tend to ping back and forth between extremes. We tend to react to whatever was the last bad thing that we encountered. So people who grew up in churches for which the gospel was for unbelievers (and then everybody else was living according to rules or principles or however this was laid out in that congregation) tend to want to move away from that and say we have the gospel. We are received in Christ. We're accepted in Christ. We believe the gospel. And so everything else just comes almost organically, reflexively, and so there's a tendency to not want to talk about pleasing God or about obeying the commandments of God. And then those people's children react to that. They say, *We really have to have holiness. Let's have rules and regulations and eclipse the gospel.*

Instead, we have both of those things. We have a gospel that frees us, and it tells us who we are in Christ. It tells us what has been done for us. But the grace that has freed us has freed us to live out a life in Christ that is defined by the Word of Christ, by what it is that he tells us to do. We believe, and because we believe we're obedient. John's book *Future Grace* (Multnomah, 2012) is one of the most helpful things in print about the fact that because we believe, we believe God has spoken to us about how we can be freed from condemnation and how we're made right. We also then believe him when he tells us what is best for us as we move toward the future that he has for us. It's both of those two things put together.

Jarvis Williams: Paul uses the language of striving in Philippians 2:12–13. "Work out your own salvation with fear and trembling." That's the language of striving, fighting, because God has worked in us. There is a consistent motif that God's work in us is the foundation underneath our striving. We strive and fight in the pursuit of holiness.

John Piper: As I've thought about this most recently, what's been helpful is to notice that the phrase "by faith" is a definer of the verb "live." For example, Galatians 2:20: "The life I now live . . . I live by faith." The living and the faith are not the same. This is the reductionism we want to avoid. The Bible says, "Strive to enter by the narrow gate." Some try to just take that word *strive* and say it means "believe harder." Well, it doesn't work that way, because you have descriptions of the Christian life that use verbs of doing or of living by faith. So faith becomes the instrument, or the empowerment, of this other thing called living or doing. "We walk by faith, not by sight." The walking is not the same as the believing. I'm walking by believing.

What that means practically is that the way the will is engaged in obedience is not simply by believing. For example, you've decided to do the command of visit this person in prison or welcome this refugee into your home, and it involves the motion of your body. The legs have to flex, and you must get up, open the door, get in the car, turn the key, take some time. These are all physical actions that have, in and of themselves, no moral significance whatsoever. But they are what you're called upon to do. They're getting you toward doing something. Now, the question is not merely believing. I must do that by faith. That's why I wrote the book *Future Grace*. What does it mean to open the door by faith, turn the key by faith, drive a car by faith, go to a prison by faith, or visit a sick person by faith? It also means your will is telling your muscles to do things. And you're doing them, and that takes some exertion that Ed rightly said is painful. It's hard to deny yourself a comfortable evening at home when you think you should go to the hospital.

Or here's where the rubber meets the road for me. The alarm goes off. I've had the grace to set it a half-hour early for meeting God in the morning. When the alarm goes off, I am absolutely dead tired. My mind and body make an absolutely compelling case for why sleep is more needful than the Bible. What do you do at that moment? By faith you get out of bed. For me that would mean believing the promise that it is more blessed to be with my Bible than to be in bed. Believe it! Having believed that, now what? Believing that will get you out of bed, but not until you say to your legs, "Flop over the edge of the bed, legs. Flop. Do it now! Do it." That really is what it comes down to when you're getting up in the morning.

After you believe, your will tells your body to do things or not. That's why I think it is over-simplistic and flattening to say that striving is only believing. It's reductionistic to say that the battle is only fought in terms of believing the gospel more or believing the promise more. It is believing the promise. Convince yourself it is more blessed. That's going to produce the motivation to get you out of bed. But then when your legs say back to you, *No. I'm not*, your will responds, *Yes, you are*. It really is interesting—you should try it sometime. You sit there, and you watch yourself talk to yourself and watch your muscles work in obedience. I mean, I just find it interesting that I can make that happen. I can say, "Go up, hand." Look at that. Phenomenal thing. Go up. It just obeys.

Ed Welch: I'm thinking two ways as you're talking, John. One is, I'm thinking theologically about striving. I talk about that, and I encourage people to do it. But then I'm also thinking personally of what happens in my own life. I'm not a good flopper. I say, okay, just put the leg out of bed, and I only win, like, a quarter of the time. I really appreciate those of you who are skilled in flopping like that. Really. I'm serious. What is it? It's the striving. This really is consistent with what you're saying, John. Striving for me, I think, is opening my eyes. *Don't you see? Don't you see who you are? Don't you see you're not your own and you're bought with a price? Don't you see who your God is? Open your eyes. Don't be deaf, dumb, and blind.* And it's that. That step, I find for myself, is utterly essential. Then it flops pretty easily.

John Piper: No, it doesn't flop easily. That is an essential step. It is absolutely an essential step because we come to believe the promises by seeing Christ for who he really is. The fight to see is the essential step. Otherwise the obedience is legalism. Getting up for your devotions is legalism if all you do is talk to your legs. But once I have seen, I still find it hard. And you said so. I'm just quoting you. It's *painful.* It's painful to do self-denial. Yes, God's commandments are not burdensome, but at that moment, there's a burdensome element. But you've preached to yourself, *It's going to be better.* You've learned this over the years. A half an hour in the Bible is going to make you a better daddy at the breakfast table. It's going to make you a better pastor. You're going to give thanks at the end of the day that you did this. Right now, though, my body is saying, *I don't want to get up.* That's why I balk at the word *easy.*

Kevin DeYoung: We can be in danger of striving, of working, of being diligent, and we can get it wrong in a couple of ways. One is to do it without faith—legalism. The other is to not be working at all the things we ought to be working at. Some people say so-and-so is a workaholic. *Dad's a workaholic because he's at the office all the time and he never comes home, and when he comes home and he has nothing left, and then he's on his phone or he's on his computer. Dad's a workaholic.* Maybe, but he's really lazy in some other areas. He's not working at all of the things that are important.

So it's not that God says just, "You don't have to work hard at a bunch of things." No. You do, but you can be working in the wrong way, not from faith, or you can be working at the wrong things or not working at all the things you should. To rest is hard work. To discipline yourself and set up those routines and have that rhythm in life where you rest can be hard work. So anyone who has the idea that part of the Christian life is going to be striving and effort and diligence, and then part of it won't, doesn't have the full-orbed view of what the Christian life is. Every part of the Christian life requires faith, and it's going to be a joy, so it's not burdensome, and then you're going to have to teach your legs to flop and it's going to be hard to do it. And it's going to be hard if you love your work, and you love the accolades that come from it, to spend time with your kids. Just saying you're working too hard is not the answer. You're not working at all the things that are most important to God.

John, some may sense a tension between Kevin's critique (in chapter 2) of single-focused sanctification and your articulation of the pursuit of joy in sanctification. Can you help us with that tension?

John Piper: Christian Hedonism says that we always want to be happy and that in all of our behavior and obedience we should be pursuing maximum joy in God. Always. No exceptions. Also, it says that every act of obedience, if it's an act of gospel obedience, should be an obedience that comes from faith. "Whatever does not proceed from faith is sin," Romans 14:23. And therefore I have a few *alwayses*. Every obedience is from faith. Every obedience is in pursuit of maximum joy.

Now, what is Kevin critiquing? It seems to me he's critiquing the *onlys*, not the *alwayses*. I was doodling as he was talking earlier, trying to draw the difference, and here's what I came up with. I'm listening to Kevin's list of forty incentives for obedience, not just one but forty—forty kinds of motivations. Things like God's wrath and imitation and duty—forty of them. I'm hearing that list, thinking, *Amen.*

Amen. Amen. They function that way for me. That's exactly the way they work. And I say, *Why? I thought you were just a joy and a faith guy. Why all these others? And why is that not a contradiction?* It's easy to get a category confusion in your head.

What I'm doing in emphasizing joy is asking, given every deed that we're called to do, what makes it a good deed, not a legalistic deed and not a deed done for show or whatever corruption can ruin the deed? What makes it a good deed? God says it's good. Anybody would say it's good biblically. But what makes it good? And my answer is that essential to the obedience is the pursuit of joy. Essential to the obedience is the reliance upon the promise—an act of faith. That's what makes it what it is. Then you have forty, fifty, a hundred kinds of things God does to help make that happen. So I'm not taking joy and putting it as one of the forty, or taking faith and putting it out here as one of the forty. I'm saying no, no. That's always there; the joy of faith is always there. That's what makes obedience to be true obedience. Then if God says I'm going to put you in hell if you don't do *that*, it works. And the *that* is rejoice.

God loves a cheerful giver. I don't regard the cheer as one of forty reasons for giving. I'm saying that's what makes the giving pleasing. Or whatever is not from faith is sin. So any act that doesn't have faith in it is sin. It's not obedience. So faith is not one of those forty. It's part of the essence of what makes the obedience to be obedience.

The point of Christian Hedonism is not to decide which of the forty incentives is most important. It's trying to decide what makes an act pleasing to God. "God is most glorified in us when we are most satisfied in him" is my way of saying every single act, in order to be maximally God-glorifying, must have in it a reliance upon all that God has done for me and what he's going to be for me, so that I am content and restful, satisfied in him and pursuing the maximum experience of that in this act. And then God can do a hundred things to help me in that from imitation to wrath to duty. Yes, just like duty. Happiness is my duty. And on and on and on. So that's the way I put it together.

Kevin DeYoung: That is exactly right and fits and melds all of that together. Just to clarify what I was saying earlier, I don't want anyone to think that they can't theologize with these incentives or that they can't sort of spin them up and drill them down and do a lot of different things with them. One of my burdens is that we not rob the unique mood of the various scriptural texts.

Scripture comes at you with the truth and with a mood, so there's a warning here. And maybe you take the warning, and 2 Peter asks, "What sort of people ought you to be in lives of holiness . . . waiting for and hastening the coming of the day of God" (3:11). You could take that and say, well, why do you want to be holy when Christ returns? Okay, because you don't want to be judged. Why don't you want to be judged? Because you want to live with him forever. And why do you want to live with him forever? Because you want to spend eternity with God. I'm happy to have all of those connections being made. What I just don't want is to rob the force of a text to hit you with the weight of a warning. I better feel something. There's a mood here, and I want to so turn every one of those angles and edges in Scripture so that it hits you with a mood. Or as a preacher or as a small-group leader, you need to massage that mood into your hearers. I just want to let Scripture speak to us with all of the specificity and all of the unique emotional force that it has for us.

John Piper: Amen. Here's an illustration from the end of 1 Corinthians 11. I just wrote a post on this a few weeks ago, because that very point clobbered me. Paul wants them to change their behavior at the Lord's Table, and so he says,

> Anyone who eats or drinks without discerning the body eats and drinks judgment on himself. That is why many of you are weak and ill, and some have died. But if we judged ourselves truly, we would not be judged. [That is, we wouldn't be sick and killed.] But when we are judged by the Lord, we are disciplined so that we may not be condemned along with the world. (vv. 29–32)

So God kills us to keep us from going to hell if we abuse the Lord's Supper—sometimes.

I can imagine a person who does not want that mood to be a part of any service. And so he just will not preach on this. He won't talk about this. He won't ever say that to his people, because he thinks that's just going to make people unhappy or depressed or discouraged or scared or lose their assurance of salvation or confused or whatever. That's exactly what I'm talking about. I love Kevin because he's just so Bible-saturated. That's why I long for you to be Bible people. So what I wrote recently was that I want to become the kind of person who feels loved by God by every way he loves me, including killing me. That's what 1 Corinthians 11 says. He makes some of us sick (and eventually dead) so that we won't be condemned with the world. That's how much he loves us. And if I don't feel loved when the Bible talks to me that way, I need to change. Not the Bible. I need to change.

I totally agree that the tone of the text, the point of the text, mustn't be muted. Yes, we want to have the whole effect of Scripture. That is one of the incentives for a happy, faith-filled experience of Communion.

Final question. Hebrews 12:14 says that there is a holiness without which we will not see the Lord. What is the meaning of that verse, and how does that relate to us being fully accepted by God on the basis of another's holiness?

Russell Moore: We're called into the life of Christ. So when Jesus dies for us and is raised from the dead for us, he joins us to himself. So someone who does not share in that life, who isn't joined to the vine—"I am the vine. You are the branches"—doesn't have Jesus's life coursing through his spiritual veins.

I thought it was interesting when John was talking about the legs flopping over the side of the bed and the mind having to speak to the legs in a person's life. That's exactly what Colossians says is going on in the corporate life of the body of Christ. The head, the energy that comes from the head, now goes to all the parts of the body. So if I am alive in Christ, then Christ's life is now coursing through me as part of the body of Christ. So if I am not experiencing that, I am not going to see the kingdom of God. It's the same kind of language the apostle Paul uses to the church at Corinth: "Do you not know that the unrighteous will not inherit the kingdom of God? But such were some of you." You share in Christ's holiness, and that works itself out in the way that you live. If that's not present, you're not alive.

Kevin DeYoung: Christ is a gift to us—Calvin said a double grace of justification and sanctification, so that you could just as soon split Christ apart as split those two things apart.

At the end of the age, when there is this call for some sort of evidence or fruit, it's not that you need to weigh out the balance; you just need something that indicates progress. It's where you're going. That's what you talked about, Ed. And it's a public vindication, I think, of both us and in a way of God at the end of the age. "Okay, here's one that's justified and going to heaven. You say there's grace abounding in him or her. Can we see a little bit of it as confirmation?" So that's a vindication of what's going on in us and also this public scene of God. God has done something in this person's life, and God is right to have justified this person through faith in Jesus, and now something to show of this glorification that will be complete was begun in this. "He who begins a good work will be faithful to complete it." And here it is. Yes, this is my child. This is one I love, and here's what I've started. And now I have every right to finish it.

John Piper: So, to boil that down, the answer to your question is this: "Pursue the holiness without which no one will see the Lord" means there is a measure of holiness required in order not to justify us but to demonstrate that we're justified, to give evidence that we are justified. And it is essential. You will be lost if you don't have evidences that you are justified. Sanctification is not optional. If you have no sanctification, you're not born of God. Those who are born of God do not continue in sin, meaning they do not give up on the fight and surrender to the flesh and say, *Once saved, always saved, I'm safe,* and live like the Devil the rest of their life, thinking eternal security means that. It doesn't. Eternal security means those whom he justified he will sanctify and, finally, glorify. And I think the reason God set it up that way is because he wants there to be a public vindication of his Spirit's powerful work in the lives of these justified people at the last day.

About the thief on the cross—this may be helpful for those of you who are worried about quantification here, because that is where you start moving. Okay, how much evidence do I have to have? The thief on the cross had a very small file of good works and a very large file of bad works. So let's just say he was forty years old. He was "saved" only two hours before he died on the cross. And I do believe he was saved, because Jesus said, "Today you'll be with me in paradise." He had thirty-nine years and three hundred, sixty-four days of bad works. Everything he did was sin up till that moment. So the file is jam-packed with bad works that are going to damn him to hell if he has to take the credit for those. And Jesus says he's going to go to heaven. And I don't believe he's exempt from the judgment according to works. So at the last judgment, as he stands there with all the condemning demons around him accusing and laughing up their sleeve at this guy, he's going to pass the judgment according to works? God opens his file cabinet and goes to the back and pulls out this little, skinny file of good works, and he says, "When I touched him on the cross, he turned to his fellow thief and rebuked him and confessed his own sin before him and humbled himself and said, 'We deserve to be here and this man's done nothing. So why are you talking like that?' And that's the evidence I will put on the table of the courtroom that he's mine." And then he burns up the rest of the file or puts it under the blood. And that's all it took.

What's required is not a quantity but a reality. Is there a reality in your life that will be able to show on the last day that you're born of God?

Ed Welch: Yes, and that can be a can of worms. That Hebrews 12:14 text is a tough one. I'm just trying to think where can I go with those things. I hear what you're saying, and I look at myself and see so many ugly things—how do I quantify good works and bad ones and have assurance I'm in good standing with God? Also there are corporate means of grace, and church discipline is one of them. And if I'm not being disciplined by my church, then isn't this evidence of their seeing the grace of God in me and my being in Christ?

Would something like the following be appropriate? I go to my elders and say, "Here's my life. Do I need to be excommunicated?" And if I'm going to a church that does church discipline and I make my life available to them, and they say, "No, you are a member of good standing in this church," I should have assurance about the verdict coming on the last day. It's not quite going where you're going with explanation of Hebrews 12:14, John, but am I allowed to bring some kind of hope like that into the explanation of this text?

John Piper: I don't understand the question.

Kevin DeYoung: Ed is saying the elders of the church have the keys of the kingdom—to bind, to loose—and that assurance is a community project. So it's significant when the elders of your church say they see evidences of grace in you. They don't see disqualifying. You are a member in good standing. In other words, the church provides a precursor of the final judgment and evaluation to come, which should give the tender conscience some assurance.

And it seems to me the other piece of this is to remember that perhaps the most precious, rare, exquisite good work before the Lord is true repentance. And it's not as if, well, everyday I just have bad works and good works all piling up. There's repentance. The Puritans said that repentance is the vomit of the soul. That is a hard, ugly, nasty thing to do. It may be that among the most beautiful splendor of holiness in our life to ornament God's gospel to say that he repented and he hated that sin. And that's a huge part of the evidence.

John Piper: That's helpful. Thank you.

John, would you close us in prayer?

John Piper: *Father, in a sense everywhere we turn there are cans of worms that if we were not helped by you at every moment we could take almost every sentence in this conference and twist it into something hurtful. And so I'm asking that you help these folks not to do that. Just may every sentence be turned in its most truthful way, its most biblical way for the greatest good for every person. So give us rest. Give us sweetness in fellowship now. May Christ be the center of all of our conversation. I pray in Jesus's name. Amen.*

Acknowledgments

Lane, Justin, Lydia, and the rest of the team at Crossway were willing to team up once again. We thank God for your diligence in proofing and publishing and for our ongoing partnership with you for the gospel.

Jon, Scott, Josh, Dave, and the rest of the team at Desiring God have done the work to put on the National Conference each fall now for ten years, the plenaries from which become these chapters. This same team does it again in the winter for our Conference for Pastors. We thank God for the energy and focus and mission of these comrades at desiringGod.org in the Great Cause of Jesus's global mission.

Noël, Talitha, Megan, Carson, Cole, and the rest of our family and closest friends know us best, put up with our sins and failings, support and sustain us, encourage us to press forward, and remind us not to outrun the supply lines. We thank God for the personal means of his grace that you are to us—sometimes the most painful kind but typically the most enjoyable.

Jesus, the perfect human image of the invisible God (Col. 1:15), you are "the Holy and Righteous One" (Acts 3:14) in whom we are, with such lavish grace, chosen and born again and justified and sanctified and glorified and more. You alone are the one to whom we are happily being conformed (Rom. 8:29) for true holiness and deepest happiness. We will ever thank God and celebrate that you loved us and gave yourself for us (Gal. 2:20). We keep leaning into you for more grace that we might daily act the miracle.

David Mathis and John Piper
Minneapolis, Minnesota
June 7, 2013

Subject Index

Name Index

Scripture Index

✳ desiring God

If you would like to explore further the vision of God and life presented in this book, we at Desiring God would love to serve you. We have thousands of resources to help you grow in your passion for Jesus Christ and help you spread that passion to others. At desiringGod.org, you'll find almost everything John Piper has written and preached, including more than sixty books. We've made over thirty years of his sermons available free online for you to read, listen to, download, and watch.

In addition, you can access hundreds of articles, find out where John Piper is speaking, and learn about our conferences. Desiring God has a whatever-you-can-afford policy, designed for individuals with limited discretionary funds. If you'd like more information about this policy, please contact us at the address or phone number below. We exist to help you treasure Jesus and his gospel above all things because *he is most glorified in you when you are most satisfied in him.* Let us know how we can serve you!

Desiring God

Post Office Box 2901 / Minneapolis, Minnesota 55402
888.346.4700   mail@desiringGod.org

A Challenge to Love with Heart *and* Mind *and* Hands

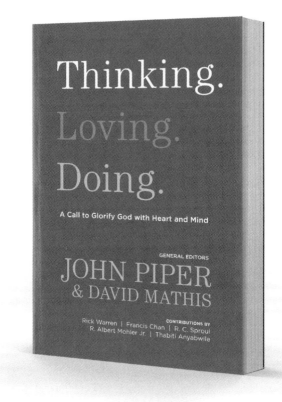

Here is a call to holistic Christianity. A challenge to be *thinkers*, engaged and serious about knowing God. And to be *feelers*, pulsing with passion for Jesus and his gospel. And to be *doers*, endeavoring great acts of love for others.

With contributions from **Rick Warren, Francis Chan, R. C. Sproul**, John Piper, **Albert Mohler**, and **Thabiti Anyabwile**, *Thinking. Loving. Doing.* extends a thorough and compelling invitation to experience the fullness of the Christian life.